The Christian Philosophy of Herman Dooyeweerd

REFORM
YOUR MIND

To my son Benja, in hope.

To write an introduction to Dooyeweerd is not an easy task. The first dive into the cold waters of his transcendental critique may lead the reader to give up. In this book, however, Josué Reichow brought us to warm waters! With a creative approach, the Dutch philosopher is introduced from different angles. Full of examples and parallels with contemporary authors this a great option to start swimming.

Guilherme de Carvalho,
Director of the Brazilian Association for Christians in Science,
and Director of Brazilian L'Abri

In concise and accessible manner L'Abri worker Josué Reichow introduces us to twentieth-century Dutch philosopher, Herman Dooyeweerd. Reichow locates Dooyeweerd in the context of modernity, summarizes key concepts within his philosophy, and illustrates the ongoing fruitfulness of his thought by way of engaging contemporary currents in the Brazilian context. This is a fine introduction that I am glad to have read and am delighted to recommend.

Mark P. Ryan,
Director of the Francis A. Schaeffer Institute,
Adjunct Professor of Religion and Culture at
Covenant Theological Seminary, St. Louis, MO (USA)

With his originally written book, Josué Reichow shows that the thinking of the Dutch philosopher Herman Dooyeweerd is by no means old-fashioned and out of date. His thinking can still inspire an up-to-date analysis of what is going on in our time. It is Reichow's merit to make this clear in an accessible narrative.

Jan Hoogland,
Associate Professor in Public Administration and Political Science in the Faculty of Social Sciences at the Vrije Universiteit Amsterdam (Free University of Amsterdam)

Josué Reichow reveals the relevance of reformational philosophy to an age found unexpectedly still in need of God. *Reform Your Mind* examines how Dooyeweerd breaks with Western orthodoxy by presenting a compelling argument for the integrality of creation, both natural and supernatural. If you want to see the depths of Christ's work of reconciliation, read this book.

Imogen Sinclair,
British political commentator and campaigner, Director of the New Social Covenant Unit.

*The Christian Philosophy
of Herman Dooyeweerd*

REFORM
YOUR MIND

JOSUÉ REICHOW

cántaro
publications

www.cantaroinstitute.org

Reform Your Mind: The Philosophy of Herman Dooyeweerd
by Josué Reichow

Published by Cántaro Publications, a publishing imprint of the Cántaro Institute, Jordan Station, ON.

© 2022 by Cántaro Institute. All rights reserved. Except for brief quotations in critical publications or reviews, no part of this book may be reproduced in any manner without prior written consent from the publishers.

Book design by Steven R. Martins

Library & Archives Canada

ISBN 978-1-990771-00-2

Printed in the United States of America

TABLE OF CONTENTS

Foreword by David T. Koyzis 7
Acknowledgments 9
Introduction 11
1.0 From Wittenberg to Paris: A Panorama of Modernity 17
   1.1 The Concept of Modernity 20
      1.1.1 The Epistemological Dimension 22
      1.1.2 The Ideal of Progress 28
      1.1.3 In its Economic Dimension: The Industrial Revolution 30
      1.1.4 The Other Pole of Modernity 32
   1.2 A Postmodernity? 34
      1.2.1 Herman Dooyeweerd and Postmodernity 38
2.0 From Geneva to Amsterdam: Dutch Neo-Calvinism as a Response to Modernity 41
   2.1 The Reform of Theoretical Thinking 47
   2.2 A Biblical View of the Heart and the Development of a Critical Philosophy 50
      2.2.1 A Private Belief? 53
3.0 What has Amsterdam to do with Athens? The Development of a Christian Philosophy 55

3.1		Philosophy and Christianity	55
	3.1.1	The Structure of Reality: Cosmonomic Modal Ontology	57
3.2		Modal Ontology	61
	3.2.1	Who is the I? Dooyeweerd's Anthropology	64
3.3		The Relationship Between Philosophy and Theology	69

4.0 What Has Babel to do with Jerusalem? The Roots of Western Culture — 75

4.1		Biologism	76
4.2		Economicism	77
4.3		Dataism	79
4.4		The Driving Force of History in Dooyeweerd	80
4.5		Religious Ground-Motives	83
	4.5.1	Matter and Form	83
	4.5.2	Creation, Fall and Redemption	86
	4.5.3	Nature and Grace	88
	4.5.4	Nature and Freedom	91

5.0 What Has Amsterdam to do with Brazil? Reflections on Christianity and Culture — 97

5.1	The Case of Brazil	98
5.2	Christians Against Culture	100
5.3	Christians of the Culture	105
5.4	Christians as Culture's Reformers	108

TABLE OF CONTENTS

6.0	A Dialogue between Amsterdam, Lausanne and Medellín: A Reformational Critique of Latin American Theology		113
	6.1	Theology of *Missão Integral* (TMI)	115
		6.1.1 Similarities and Tensions between TMI and Neo-Calvinism	118
	6.2	Liberation Theology	123
		6.2.1 The Reformational Critique of Liberation Theology	127
	6.3	The Dualism of Nature and Grace	128
	6.4	The Problem of Praxis and Historicism	130
	6.5	The Socio-Analytical Mediation (SAM)	131
7.0	Final Considerations		135
About the Author			139

FOREWORD

I FIRST DISCOVERED the writings of Dutch Christian philosopher Herman Dooyeweerd in the mid 1970s when I was an undergraduate student. I quickly discovered that he was not easy to read, as his ideas seemed buried in a turgid prose style. Nevertheless, the hard work I put into understanding his philosophy more than paid off with respect to the use to which I discovered I could put it. My chosen academic field was political science, and I found that his nonreductionist approach to public life simply made sense. It better accounted for the realities of political life than, for example, so-called realists or behaviourists who could make sense of only a particular facet of reality. A decade later I would go on to write a dissertation on Dooyeweerd at the University of Notre Dame, a process that thoroughly grounded me in his magnum opus, *A New Critique of Theoretical Thought*. Because his Philosophy of the Law-Idea so well accounts for the fulness of God's world, it became a primary influence on my own writings, including *Political Visions and Illusions* (Downers Grove, IL: IVP Academic, 2019).

Half a century ago, Dooyeweerd was largely unknown outside certain rarified circles associated with the Dutch Reformed tradition. But in the decades since his passing, more of his works have been translated into English and other languages, most notably Portuguese. These translations have not necessarily made him easier to comprehend, but once readers have immersed themselves in his philosophy, acquainting themselves with the specialized terms that make up the building blocks of his system, they will encounter a treasury of insights into the nature of the cosmos—insights that can be applied in a variety of academic fields as well as in lived experience.

One of the more remarkable developments in recent decades is the dissemination of Dooyeweerd's thought, along with other neocalvinist or reformational writings, in Brazil, the fifth largest country in the world and still for now a predominantly Catholic nation. The book you hold in your hands is written by one such Brazilian whom I have the pleasure to know through English l'Abri. Josué Reichow here introduces us to the principal contours of Dooyeweerd's philosophy, originally for a Brazilian readership and now, in translation, for an English-speaking audience.

Others have written introductions to Dooyeweerd's thought, but this is the only one in English that I know of which treats his growing influence in Brazil, bringing him into conversation with Liberation Theology and the Integral Mission of the Lausanne Movement. The rapid growth of evangelicalism in Brazil has astounded Christians in the northern hemisphere, especially in North America and Europe, where the faith appears to be declining. Of course, when such large numbers of people turn to Christ for their salvation, the fruits of their conversions do not automatically manifest themselves, especially with respect to the health of the larger society. Yet the fact that an increasing number of Brazilians are reading the likes of Dooyeweerd is a hopeful sign. It means that they are carefully thinking through the implications of their faith and genuinely seeking the will of God as they live their lives to his glory. I trust that Reichow's book will serve a growing audience interested in Dooyeweerd's important contribution to the enrichment of Christian intellectual life.

David T. Koyzis, Global Scholars Canada
February 2022

ACKNOWLEDGEMENTS

THIS BOOK IS AN EXPRESSION of the gift economy in which we all participate in. Without the people and the institutions that I herewith mention – and many more not named – this work would not have been possible.

I am grateful for my wife, Lili, and her constant support and encouragement, as well as the space she carved out so I could have the time to work on this book. Thank you for your love and care.

I am thankful for my editor and publisher Steven R. Martins, who, since our first contact, has been an encourager. Thank you for taking up the challenge of revising, editing, and improving the translation of this book.

I am grateful for the work of my two colleagues and friends, Guilherme de Carvalho and Rodolfo Amorim Souza, for introducing to me, and to the Brazilian public more broadly, Dooyeweerd, as well as being examples of faith, work, and hope in Christ.

I thank the Association for Reformational Philosophy for being so generous towards me, making it possible for me to have attended two Reformational Philosophy Conferences (Amsterdam, 2011 and Leuven, 2016) as I immersed myself within this tradition.

Special thanks to all my colleagues at English L'Abri, who supported me throughout this time, and who have been good partners in philosophical debate.

I also want to thank a few people who contributed to this book, either through fruitful conversation or by practical and intellectual encouragement: Andrew Fellows, Edith Reitsema, Dick Goodwin, Rudolf von Sinner, Rodomar Ramlow, Philip and Miriam Sampson.

I am grateful to the Lord God Creator and Redeemer of all things. I am thankful for the gift of reflection.

Soli Deo Gloria

INTRODUCTION

THE BOOK YOU HOLD in your hands is not addressed solely to philosophers, but to everyone who wishes to develop a Christian perspective, not only of philosophy, but of the humanities and sciences; and for those who are interested in the ways of integrating their faith with academic production and reflection on the various aspects of reality. The foundation on which this work stands is the affirmation of Christ's complete Lordship over all areas of created reality. There is nothing in creation that is not being reconciled by the death and resurrection of Jesus Christ, whether thrones or powers, rulers or authorities, epistemologies or ontologies.

It seems to me that the categories of reflection developed by the reformational philosophy of Dooyeweerd have the potential to impact the various spheres of our societies towards a reformation of thought that is reflected in at least three distinct fields: (i) *academic production*, whether philosophical or scientific; (ii) the *local church*, especially in the development of a *public theology*; and more broadly, (iii) Christian *cultural engagement*.

In the western academic context, the dogma of the religious autonomy of reason is still present. According to the Amsterdam philosopher, this perspective is one of the main characteristics of modernity, which propagates the idea that religious beliefs are strictly related to a private sphere of life and that intellectual production has nothing to do with these beliefs. For this and other reasons, universities have developed an anti-religious and, I dare say, particularly, an anti-Christian environment. Thus, the presentation of a reformational philosophy in this book can provide a strong analytical framework to challenge this perspective.

Regarding the impact of Dooyeweerd's ideas on the church, I would say that there is still a strong dualism at work in many Christian settings. Many Christians see the advancement of knowledge as something unimportant, worldly, and even sinful and, thus, they exempt themselves from any activity that does not necessarily involve the ecclesiastical structure. On the other hand, many Christians in academia, eager to bear witness of their faith, often end up internalizing theoretical perspectives that clash with the Christian faith because they do not have a critical Christian framework that allows them to read theories and concepts in the light of their faith.

A few years ago, I participated in a lecture and debate with academic Christians about the challenges of Christian witness in the university. I was surprised by the perspective presented there: the university was reduced, exclusively, to a mission field, in which souls must be rescued for the church. The university did not seem to have legitimacy on its own. The Dooyeweerdian perspective stands in opposition to this sort of dualism, offering a bridge to an integral perspective of life.

Similarly, the perspective developed by Herman Dooyeweerd can shed light on the debate about the modes of interaction between Christian faith and culture. It seems to me that this point is especially important for Christians engaged in the field of art. How do we understand the little importance given by the church to artistic production and artists themselves? How do we read/interpret art in order to understand our times? The reformational perspective provides the philosophical and theological framework for the affirmation of a

INTRODUCTION

Christian faith absolutely engaged in culture, insofar as it recognizes it as a *locus* of God's glory and, therefore, legitimate in itself.

Besides these potential contributions in different areas, this book serves as an introduction to Herman Dooyeweerd's philosophy, as I introduce him in the context of modernity as well as in the setting of the Dutch theological movement in which he was brought up.

Herman Dooyeweerd was born in 1894 in Amsterdam, at a time that many consider the apogee of modernity, which would soon be shaken by the advent of the First (1914-1918) and Second World War (1939-1945). From a very early age, he professed the Christian faith, having within his family, especially his father, the profound influence of Abraham Kuyper and the Dutch neo-Calvinist movement. The young Dooyeweerd, as a result, studied law at the university founded by Kuyper, the Free University of Amsterdam.

At the Free University Dooyeweerd taught philosophy, history and law for 40 years. He was a member of the Royal Dutch Academy of Sciences, considered one of the most influential authors in the Netherlands. Dooyeweerd died in 1977, the same year that Hans Rookmaaker died – a Dooyeweerdian art historian, who had been the founder of the art history department at the same university, as well as the founder of the Dutch L'Abri. The contemporary influence of Dooyeweerd's thought transcends Dutch territory, reaching the rest of Europe, the USA, Canada, South Africa, and particularly Brazil with its growing evangelicalism. In fact, chapters 5 and 6 serve as case studies of a Dooyeweerdian approach to culture and political theology, respectively, in the Brazilian context.

Therefore, in order to present Dooyeweerd's philosophy and its possible applications, this book is divided into six chapters. In the opening chapter, called *From Wittenberg to Paris: A Panorama of Modernity*, I paint a general picture of what is understood by modernity, as Dooyeweerd interacts with and responds to the philosophy of that period. I use authors from various fields of knowledge to set up a kind of background against which the Dutch author's thought can be presented afterwards.

In the second chapter, named *From Geneva to Amsterdam: Dutch Neo-Calvinism as a Response to Modernity*, I introduce the intellectual context in which Dooyeweerd grew up and developed his thinking. I begin the chapter by presenting Dutch neo-Calvinism, especially in the figure of Abraham Kuyper, and its developments as a movement, with its influence going far beyond the Netherlands itself. Then I present the central element of the Dooyeweerdian project, namely his critique of modern thought, expressed in the privatization of faith and in the dogma of the religious neutrality of reason.

The third chapter, *What has Amsterdam to do with Athens? The Development of a Christian Philosophy*, is a more detailed exposition of the core ideas of his Reformational philosophy. In it, I discuss the relationship between philosophy and Christianity, emphasizing Dooyeweerd's project of a Christian philosophy. Then, I approach the concepts of: the *cosmonomic idea*, *sphere-sovereignty*, and *modal ontology*. I conclude the chapter by discussing Dooyeweerdian *anthropology* and his understanding of the relationship between *philosophy and theology*.

In the next chapter, *What Has Babel to do with Jerusalem? The Roots of Western Culture*, I address the ways of understanding history, initially dealing with examples of reductionisms from biology, sociology and technology. Then I introduce the Dooyeweerdian concept of religious ground-motives, discussing Dooyeweerd's way of interpreting the history and development of Western culture from four ground-motives: (i) the Greek matter and form; (ii) the Christian creation, fall and redemption; (iii) the Scholastic nature and grace; and (iv) the Modern nature and freedom.

The fifth chapter, called *What Has Amsterdam to do with Bra-*

INTRODUCTION

zil? Reflections on Christianity and Culture, discusses the relationship between Christianity and culture in the Brazilian context, utilizing different relationship models, such as *Christians against culture* and *Christians of culture*, reflecting on concrete examples and developments of these models in the Brazilian setting, and then presenting the insights of reformational tradition on the subject, expressed in the model of *Christians as culture's reformers*.

In the sixth and last chapter of this book, *A Dialogue between Amsterdam, Lausanne and Medellín: A Reformational Critique of Latin American Theology*, I seek to establish a dialogue between three traditions of political theology: Dooyeweerd 's *Reformational Tradition*, *Teologia da Missão Integral* (Theology of Integral Mission) and *Liberation Theology*, reading the latter two in light of the first. I begin the chapter with an outline of these two perspectives developed in Latin America, and then I address the points of convergence and divergence with the reformational perspective in an attempt to initiate a dialogue between these traditions.

My hope is that this work could contribute meaningfully towards the formation of an intellectual community that would build a robust perspective of thought, grounded in the foundations of the Christian faith and that serves as an instrument for human flourishing in all aspects of life and created reality, as our whole being and our minds are reformed by the mind of Christ.

1

FROM WITTENBERG TO PARIS: A PANORAMA OF MODERNITY

WE LIVE IN A POST-EVERYTHING WORLD: post-traditional, post-industrial, post-Christian, post-binary, post-colonial, and post-human. Name something in the past and you will quickly find someone telling you that we have moved beyond it.

In order to understand anything post-, especially *postmodernity*, it is necessary to say something about its most famous suffix: *modernity*. What is modernity? What bearing does it have on how we make sense of the world and how we live our lives? These are fundamental questions for anyone who wants to understand our culture and integrate the Christian faith.

We cannot understand our current era of postmodernity without understanding modernity. But anyone who has dug this far will quickly find that modernity is inseparable from the historical period before it, the so-called *Middle Ages*. It will soon become clear that understanding culture means understanding *history* – and history does not interpret itself. This is where things can get quite tricky.

Every historical interpretation implies a particular view, not only of the past, but of the present and the future. It requires a reference point that would provide meaning and coherence to its explanation. In other words, history needs a *worldview*[1] from which a set of references would come, in order to guide its interpretive process.

The past is a theoretical battlefield. Think about a relatively recent historical event, like the *Woodstock Festival* in 1969 in the United States. Was it a symbol of freedom and liberation or a symbol of a lost generation? It depends on who you ask! Though the objective reality of that event does not change, its interpretation and meaning do, because they are informed by a set of references that we call "worldviews."

Here is another way of putting it: *our view of history is not neutral*. There is no such thing as an objective view of history. C. S. Lewis, in his inaugural lecture as Professor and Chair of Medieval and Renaissance Literature at Cambridge University, stated:

> All lines of demarcation between what we call 'periods' should be subject to constant revision. Would that we could dispense with them altogether. As a great Cambridge historian said: "Unlike dates, periods are not facts. They are retrospective conceptions that we form about past events, useful to focus discussion, but very often leading historical thought astray" [...] Unfortunately, however, as historians we cannot give up periods [...] We cannot hold together huge masses of

---

1. From the German *Welantschauung*. The term was employed by Immanuel Kant (1724-1804) becoming extremely popular within the German Romantic movement of the 19th century. In the Humanities the term gained special attention in the works of Wilhelm Dilthey (1833-1911).

particulars without putting into them some kind of structure.²

We must ask questions about the categorizations of historical periods without discarding them completely, as if they had no analytical validity. They do say something about a concrete past event or era, but also something about the contemporary ways of understanding the world.

Why begin this introduction to Dooyeweerd's philosophy by exploring the concept of modernity?

In the first place, Dooyeweerdian philosophy and its subsequent tradition was in constant critical dialogue with modernity and the way of thinking that had developed within it, notably with the philosophers of the Enlightenment. Those who wish to understand the philosophical construction established by the Dutch thinker must have a framework to comprehend modernity and its consequences, especially within philosophy and social theory.

Secondly, modernity represents an explicit challenge to Christianity, giving it a character that is at least secondary in relation to questions concerning public life and the scientific and philosophical enterprise. The development of a Christian philosophy necessarily requires a dialogue with, and a challenge to modernity's philosophical paradigms.

Thirdly, a reformational philosophy like that of Herman Dooyeweerd can equip those who work within the field of humanities with strong theoretical categories of thought, which in turn could shed light on current debates from a Christian perspective.

---

2. C. S Lewis, "De description temporum." In: They Asked for a Paper (London: Geoffrey Bles, 1962), 11.

1.1 The Concept of Modernity

To speak of modernity is to speak of a *worldview*[3], a way of perceiving reality, that emerged in Europe in the XVI century and, with time, increased in both form and scope. The term *modernity* refers to "a comprehensive designation of all the changes - intellectual, social and political - that created the modern [contemporary] world."[4]

Five historical events were paradigmatic, as they illustrated these changes: the Reformation, the Renaissance, the Enlightenment, the French Revolution and the Industrial Revolution. In this sense, the modern era could be understood as a process of radical transformation of previous patterns of order and social relations. Modernity has implanted new patterns of ideals, philosophical and political thought, economics, aesthetics, and religion.

Furthermore, when it comes to modernity, it is a commonplace in the humanities to speak of the growing separation between religion and other spheres of life. As the Lutheran theologian Wilhelm Wachholz states: "In pre-modern times, religion permeated the entire life of societies. The modern separation between religion and the secular world was not known."[5] The Catholic philosopher Charles Taylor coined the term *immanent frame*[6] to refer to one of the consequences of the process of secularization in the West, expressing the denial of any categories which could transcend the natural world.

---

3. See Rodolfo Amorim, "Cosmovisão: evolução do conceito e aplicação cristã." In: Guilherme de Carvalho, Maurício Cunha e Cláudio Antônio Cardoso Leite (Org.), *Cosmovisão cristã e transformação* (Viçosa: Ultimato, 2006), 41.
4. Krishan Kumar, *Da sociedade pós-industrial à pós-moderna: Novas teorias sobre o mundo contemporâneo* (Rio de Janeiro: Zahar, 1997), 79.
5. Wilhelm Wachholz, *História e teologia da reforma: introdução* (São Leopoldo: Sinodal, 2010), 14.
6. Cf. Charles Taylor, *A Secular Age* (Harvard University Press), 2007.

In this respect, the *Protestant Reformation,* sparked by Martin Luther in 1517, was an important (proto) modern event, allowing space for a process of individualization and appealing to personal responsibility. The Reformation would later reach vast territories in Europe and gain many adherents.[7]

In another passage, commenting on the Reformation, Wacholz states that:

> [...] the Reformation inaugurated Christianity as a principle of adherence to a Christian community. In modernity, as the church and the state split, as accomplished by the French Revolution of 1789, religion is no longer the foundation of society. The state and the market become these foundations. Societies are now organized according to the State and the market. Society is now made up of "atheistic" people, with Christian people among them. Religion becomes an option.[8]

Modernity's transformation of religion from public to private is just one of its many transformations. Modernity transforms everything. To restrict it to one aspect reduces its analytical and explanatory potential. For the British sociologist Anthony Giddens, modernity, "[...] refers to the style, custom of life or social organization that emerged in Europe from the 17th century and that later became more or less worldwide in its influence."[9] This association of modernity with *change* is a rare consensus within social theory.

As the title of Marshal Berman's book suggests, *All That is Solid*

---

7. See Carter Lindberg, *As Reformas na Europa* (São Leopoldo: Sinodal, 2001), p. 114. Protestantism is characterized, therefore, by a strong appeal to individuality and personal responsibility. Cf. also Max Weber, *A ética protestante e o espírito do capitalismo* (São Paulo: Companhia das Letras, 2004).
8. Wilhelm Wachholz, *História e teologia da reforma*, 14.
9. Anthony Giddens, *As consequências da modernidade* (São Paulo: Editora Unesp, 1991), 11.

Melts into Air. Modernity "dumps us all in a whirlwind of permanent disintegration and change, of struggle and contradiction, of ambiguity and anguish."[10] The entire existing order, whether religious, political, social, economic, cultural, or aesthetical, has been replaced by a new order and new ways of conceiving reality.

What are these changes and transformations? In order to answer this question, two dimensions of change must be analyzed: firstly, the *epistemological dimension*; and the *ideal of progress*. A brief reflection on the emergence of *post-modernity* will then follow.

1.1.1 The Epistemological Dimension
Rationalization

If there is a dominant image of modernity, it is that of a rational, mathematized, measured and meticulously observed world, seen through the eyes of reason. Rationality, allegedly foregrounded in medieval Christianity, emerged as the most reliable source of knowledge, as a parameter and epistemological basis for a *disenchanted world.*[11] Modern people move their eyes from heaven and place them on the earth alone.

Against this dominant perception, we must carefully note that the epistemology emerging from modernity is closer to rationalism than to any "emergence" of rationality. To claim that reason arises in the modern period is to deny the capacity of reason for both medieval *patristics* and *scholasticism,* as well as for the ancient Greeks. Take for instance the political works of Marsilius of Padua, a contemporary of Thomas Aquinas, which, by exposing his method in the work *Defensor Pacis*, elaborates his ideas from a clear ideal of rationality when he states: "[...] I will divide this work into three parts. Using correct

---

10. Marshall Berman, *Tudo que é sólido se desmancha no ar: a aventura da modernidade* (São Paulo: Companhia das Letras, 2007), 24.
11. Max Weber, *A ética protestante e o espírito do capitalismo*, 88.

methods developed by *reason* and supported by well-established and self-evident propositions."[12]

Aquinas, the most famous of the *scholastic* authors, made the great medieval synthesis between Christian theology and Aristotle, even developing the idea of *natural reason,* which would be free to know and unveil the structure of creation. Aquinas attributed an important role to rationality in his theological and philosophical system.[13] Rationality is not a modern novelty. Modernity's key innovation is the circumscription of all forms of knowledge to reason, disregarding both tradition and the idea of revelation, both of which are present within Christianity.

For the French sociologist Alain Touraine, "[modernity] is the diffusion of the products of rational, scientific and technological activity",[14] and this is driven by the rational person. Touraine claims that one cannot speak of modern society if divine revelation persists. Modernity, therefore, is characterized by the displacement of a religious centre of explaining reality, one that is permeated by faith, to a rational centre, strictly human and erected under the pillars of science.

At the genesis of this epistemological turn, two philosophers of great influence stand out: the French René Descartes (1596-1650) and the German Immanuel Kant (1724-1804).

Modern philosophy had its starting point with *Descartes' Discourse on Method.* The complete title is of great illustrative value: *Discourse on the Method of Rightly Conducting One's Reason and of Seeking*

---

12. Marsílio de Pádua, *O defensor da paz* (Petrópolis: Vozes, 1995), 73.
13. Herman Dooyeweerd, *Raízes da cultura ocidental: as opções pagã, secular e cristã* (São Paulo: Cultura Cristã, 2015), 45-46.
14. Alain Touraine, *Crítica da modernidade* (Petrópolis, RJ: Vozes, 1994), 17.

Truth in the Sciences. For Descartes, rational thought is the only safe source of knowledge in the world. With his famous *Cogito ergo sum*, "I think, therefore I am", he establishes methodical doubt as a way of knowing. According to Leslie Newbigin:

> Descartes lived in a time of scepticism. It inaugurated the intellectual revolution of the seventeenth century and laid the foundations for what we now think of as the "modern" scientific age. [He] was convinced that by following the method adopted [...] it would be possible to have more than what we would call a *mere belief*, but, on the contrary, we would have certainties, a *precise knowledge*.[15]

In the words of Fritjof Capra:

> [Descartes] doubts everything he can submit to doubt – all traditional knowledge, the impressions of his senses and even the fact of having a body – and he comes to something he cannot doubt, the existence of himself as thinker. [...] Hence Descartes deduced that the essence of human nature resides in thought [...].[16]

Science, in this respect, cannot consider any knowledge that is not based on a rigorous, methodical rational process. The radical introduction of this new conception of science in modernity is understood as a revolution. All knowing needed to be changed. This new epistemology found echoes in existing paradigms of science, such as the *mechanistic* models of Isaac Newton, considered the father of modern science; the *organicist* models of Herbert Spencer; the *evolutionary* theory of Charles Darwin; and that of *positivism* of Augusto Comte, who would have a strong influence in both France and Brazil.

---

15. Lesslie Newbigin, *Discovering Truth in a Changing World* (London: Alpha International, 2003), 4.

16. Fritjof Capra, *O ponto de mutação: a ciência, a sociedade e a cultura emergente* (São Paulo: Círculo do Livro, 1982), 54.

Another central figure in modernity is, without a doubt, the German philosopher Immanuel Kant. Vast and complex, Kant's philosophy is called a *critical philosophy*. One of his main works was published in 1781 under the title of *A Critique of Pure Reason*. It contains an extensive response to the English empiricist philosophy of John Locke and David Hume. Defending an *a priori* knowledge and reason as a *starting point* for knowledge, at the expense of experience, Kant argues that:

> Experience is by no means the only field to which our understanding can be confined. Experience tells us what it is, but not that it must necessarily be what it is [...]. It never gives us, therefore, general truths; and our *reason*, which is particularly anxious for this kind of *knowledge*, is caused by it, and not satisfied. General truths, which at the same time bring the character of an earlier need, must be independent of experience - clear and certain in themselves.[17]

The place of religion in Kant's philosophy is also discussed in *Religion Within the Limits of Reason*, in which the emphasis is on the central place of rationality as an interpretative parameter of any reality. Kant's conception of rationality is too elaborate and complex to be expressed succinctly. It will suffice to say that religion has a secondary role in the Kantian project of a universal morality. As Durant puts it, commenting on Kant's work "[...] churches and dogmas are only valuable insofar as they help the moral development of the race."[18]

Thus, theology displaced in the public sphere from primacy is given to other disciplines of knowledge, such as philosophy or sociology. In the classical conception of modernity, there is no room

---

17. Kant apud Will Durant, *A história da filosofia* (São Paulo: Nova Cultural, 2000), 256.

18. *Ibid.*, 267.

for a public theology.

In this way, one of the main characteristics generated with the advent of modernity is *rationalization*. Reason is legitimated as a herald of truth. As Touraine puts it: "[modernity] is above all the construction of a rationalist image of the world that integrates man in nature, the microcosm and the macrocosm, and that rejects all forms of dualism of the body and soul, of the human world of transcendence."[19]

Human persons now begin to see the world as something rational. The modern world becomes strictly logical. It can be known, researched, studied, and explored by a reason instrumentalized by science. If there is logic, there are necessarily invariant patterns, which moderns call *laws*. Now, if there were physical laws that governed the universe, why wouldn't there be laws that governed nature, social relations and even the human person?

Science quickly began to consolidate itself in modernity as the way of knowing the laws of an ordered and logical world. For such an undertaking, the use of reason became a fundamental condition. As anthropologists Eriksen and Nielsen suggest:

> If mathematics, the language of reason, could reveal fundamental natural truths like Newton's laws, did it not follow that nature was itself rational and that every enterprise directed by reason would be destined for success?[20]

This radical change in modern epistemology is one cause of the whirlwind that Marshall Berman tells us about. When the "[...] great discoveries in the physical sciences [...] occurred, a change in our im-

---

19. Alain Touraine, *Crítica da modernidade*, 37.
20. Thomas Hylland Eriksen e Finn Sivert Nielsen, *História da antropologia* (Petrópolis, RJ: Vozes, 2007), 19.

age of the universe and of place that we occupy in it was affected."[21] Our worldview was altered from all pre-modern forms. As stated by Giddens: "[...] modernity radically changes the nature of everyday social life and affects the most personal aspects of our experience."[22]

Subjectivation

Despite what has been discussed thus far, it is important to note that modernity cannot be limited to the process of rationalization alone. To proceed in this way would be to make the mistake of identifying modernity with its ideology, with the pretentious idea that the "lights" of the Enlightenment came to illuminate the "darkness",[23] and that the fall of the Bastille and the ideal of the rebels of the French Revolution was the only truly modern ideal in history.

Thus, even in the very French tradition of the social sciences, called the *sociology of experience*, there are authors such as Alain Touraine and François Dubet,[24] who disagree with the interpretation of modernity as strictly identified with the process of rationalization. For them, there is another dimension that cannot in any way be excluded, namely, *subjectification*. According to Touraine's definition:

---

21. Marshall Berman, *Tudo que é sólido se desmancha no ar*, 25.
22. Anthony Giddens, *Modernidade e identidade* (Rio de Janeiro: Zahar, 2002), 9.
23. Gertrude Himmelfarb, *The Roads to Modernity:* The British, French and American Enlightenment, Vintage Books, London, 2008. In this work, the American historian defends the idea of multiple enlightenments, arguing that in the USA and as well as in the UK there were enlightenments prior to the French one. Besides, they were very different from the revolutionary ideal present in France, having at their core a conservative shape.
24. They are contemporary French sociologists connected to a school of thought know as *Sociology of* action, which emphasises the dimension of the individual experience – subjectivity – in the construction and formation of society.

[modernity is the] growing separation of the *objective* world, created by reason in accordance with the laws of nature, from the world of *subjectivity*, which is first of all that of individualism or, more precisely, that of an appeal to personal freedom.[25]

This conception emphasizes the development of the idea of the *subject*, which could not be reduced, exclusively, to its rational dimension, but which is considered an autonomous agent before society. This tradition emphasizes, therefore, the dimension of the individual, in the classic sociological duality of *agency* and *structure*. This emphasis on the free and autonomous subject is what Dooyeweerd calls the *ideal of personality*, which was born in the Renaissance and which from the beginning conflicted with the idea of *nature*.

1.1.2 The Ideal of Progress
In Its Political Dimension: The French Revolution

Within the pre-modern conception, history was conceived as being cyclical. *There is nothing new under the sun*[26] illustrates that belief of a repetition that always happens within time. According to Kumar, modernity secularized the Christian conception of time, since Christianity renews the idea of time and history, giving them meaning. In his words: "[Christianity] overthrew the naturalist conception of the ancient world, [where] there was change, but not newness."[27] The image of a modern man's march through history gains strength, and modernity is a "[...] central moment in our history, when we think entirely in historical terms."[28]

In that direction, the event that took place in France in the 18th

---

25. Alain Touraine, *Crítica da modernidade*, 12.
26. See Ecclesiastes 1:9b.
27. Krishan Kumar, *Da sociedade pós-industrial à pós-moderna*, 80.
28. Alain Touraine, *Crítica da modernidade*, p. 70.

century is a milestone of modernity, especially in terms of the idea of revolution itself, because:

> The French Revolution of 1789 was the first modern revolution. It transformed the concept of revolution. Revolution no longer meant the turning of a wheel or a cycle that always returns to its starting point. At that moment, it began to mean the creation of something entirely new, something never seen before in the world[...].[29]

One of the main consequences of the French Revolution is that it introduced the idea of a historical agent, in the sense of someone who is capable of changing the course of history. The modern person comes to see himself as someone who affects time, transforming it. Therefore, the possibilities become more open and the belief in humanity's progress increases more and more.

When dealing with the French Revolution, Berman states:

> With it and its reverberations, a large and modern audience comes to life, abruptly and dramatically. This audience shares the feeling of living in a revolutionary era, an era that unleashes explosive upheavals at all levels of personal, social, and political life.[30]

Political revolutions, economic transformations, development of science, discoveries overseas, philosophical thinking with new ideas: the human being is at the centre of history and freedom is a value that begins to flourish. This is the modern scenario, in which its expectation for the progress of humanity is growing, in which its prophets give way to scientists, and redemption by faith gives way to evolution by science. Modernity, then, became identified as the reference point of the historical evolution, and all progress was scaled

---

29. Krishan Kumar, *Da sociedade pós-industrial à pós-moderna*, 92.
30. Marshall Berman, *Tudo que é sólido se desmancha no ar*, 26.

on the axis that goes from tradition to modernity.[31]

French sociologist François Dubet asserts that societies were ranked according to their degree of modernity, whether in the rationalization of the world in Weber, in the development of productive forces in Marx, or in the division of labor in Dürkheim.[32] This process is also evident in the emergence of anthropology with its evolutionary stages – also called *comparative method* – which classifies societies from barbaric to civilized.

This consolidates a characteristic of modernity, the concentration on the future rather than on the past. In a sense, the authority of the past over the present is abolished – the *end of tradition*. It brings an atmosphere of new events, new possibilities: progress. There is a process of the *colonization of the future* – when the events to come are more relevant to the understanding of the present than the events of the past.

1.1.3 In Its Economic Dimension: The Industrial Revolution

I hope it is clear by this point that modernity is not confined to a single aspect or to a defining characteristic, but it refers to a series of transformations in the entire social order. The other dimension that must be discussed now is its economic one. If it were necessary to think of another image of the modern world it would be of a mechanized factory, a machine constantly running with steam.

It was with the Industrial Revolution of the 18th century, in Great Britain, that modernity received its material dimension. How to define this revolution? For historian Eric Hobsbawm, "[the Industrial Revolution is the] rapid, constant, and even unlimited,

---

31. Anthony Giddens, *As consequências da modernidade*, 22.
32. François Dubet, *A sociologia da experiência* (Lisboa: Instituto Piaget, 1994), 53.

multiplication of men, goods and services."³³ It brings with it a new economic model and a new way of organizing production, which is capitalism, defined by Giddens, as "[...] a goods production system centred in the relationship between the private ownership of capital and waged labour without ownership, this relationship forming the main axis of a class system."³⁴

The industrialization process resulting from the Industrial Revolution was linked to the development of technology and to the advances in science that drove modernity. In the same way, the ideal of progress catalyzed this new economic system. Regarding this notion, Polanyi observes that: "[...] animated by an emotional faith in spontaneity, the common sense attitude towards change has been replaced by an immediate mystical acceptance of the social consequences of economic progress, whatever they may be."³⁵

In addition to providing modernity its material dimension, the industrialization process also stands out because it made the West a global civilization. It is undeniable that the production system born with the Industrial Revolution has become a world economic system in which its characteristic is to constantly revolutionize the means of production. In this sense, Kumar recalls that:

> If Napoleon's armies took the ideas of the French Revolution all over Europe, the British and French navies carried the message of the Industrial Revolution all over the world. The message was simple: in our times, modern times, there is only one way to survive: to industrialize [...]. To modernize was to industrialize.³⁶

---

33. Eric J. Hobsbawm, *A era das revoluções: Europa 1789-1848* (Rio de Janeiro, Paz e Terra, 1977), 50.
34. Anthony Giddens, *As consequências da modernidade*, 61.
35. Karl Polanyi, *A grande transformação: as origens de nossa época* (Rio de Janeiro: Campus, 2000), 51.
36. Krishan Kumar, *Da sociedade pós-industrial à pós-moderna*, 94, 95.

Whether the capitalist system was praised and appreciated, as it was by the liberals of the 19th century, or even by the neoliberals of the 20th century, whether it was criticized, as it was harshly by theorists like Marx in the 19th century, coming to be called the "satanic mill" by Karl Polanyi, it is undeniably the system that was established with modernity. As such, it gained a worldwide scope, making the modern economy a completely globalized economy, impossible to think of as outside a global network.

1.1.4 The Other Pole of Modernity

It is important to note that modernity as a *rationalizing project* received several critiques beyond the field of philosophy and social theory. One of the most well-known forms of contesting modernity was *German Romanticism*[37] at the end of the 18th century. In addition to that, there was also a cultural movement called *modernism*, which took place mainly in literature and the arts. Both movements caused a separation between the social and political dimensions of modernity and its aesthetic concept.

> On the one hand, science, reason, progress, industrialism; on the other, their refutation and rejection, in favour of feeling, intuition and the use of imagination.[38]

This separation was articulated by Dooyeweerd in terms of a tension between *nature* and *freedom*.

Among the authors who research this period beyond the scientific and philosophical field, one of the most studied writers is the Frenchman Charles Baudelaire (1821-1867), mainly because of his

---

37. Movement that influenced different fields of knowledge, from philosophy to the arts. It was characterized by a strong critique of the enlightenment rationality and an emphasis on the subjectivity.

38. Krishan Kumar, *Da sociedade pós-industrial à pós-moderna*, 96.

work *The Painter of Modern Life,* written in 1863. In it, Baudelaire exposes the questions and anxieties present in the life of modern man. The ambiguity appears as follows: while he criticizes modernity, the condition of being a modern individual – capable of criticizing his own social order – is exalted, as if the act of contesting constituted an authentically modern act.

In Baudelaire's work, elements subversive to classical modernity are found. Thus:

> [reason] was fought by imagination, artifice by nature, objectivity by subjectivity, calculation by spontaneity, the mundane by the visionary, the world view of science by the appeal to the fantastic and the supernatural.[39]

In modernism there is an appeal to human freedom. In this sense, reason itself is fought, as it would obstruct human choice.

It is also necessary to remember that the European context, mainly of the 19th century was a context of radical transformations, not only political and economic, but also structural, with the growth of cities due to the industrialization process. People started to live in big cities, with an increasing complexity of social life. There was, therefore, in this process, a need for humans to (re)consider their own condition. Thus, artists and writers began to capture this new environment and to express their views.

Another important writer who stands out for developing a strong critique of modernity is the Russian Fiódor Dostoiévski (1821-1881), mainly in the book *Notes from the Underground,* published in 1864. In it, through its central character, the author utters against the ideal of progress led by science and against the reduction of man to a machine, the mere gear of a system. In a famous passage, the writer

---

39. Krishan Kumar, *Da sociedade pós-industrial à pós-moderna*, 97.

says that "[...] men continue to be men, not piano keys [...]."[40] Still on that, he says: "Even if it turns out that he is in fact a piano key, even if it is shown to him by the natural sciences and mathematics, he will not come to his senses and will purposely do something opposite, solely out of ingratitude; in fact, to impose his *will*."[41]

Later in the same work, he writes:

> If you say that all of this can also be calculated by the table – chaos, darkness, curse, so that the mere possibility of previous calculation stops everything and reason triumphs - then in that case man will be purposefully mad, to be deprived of reason and defend his opinion! I believe that. I answer for that, because every human question comes down to man constantly proving to himself that he is a man, and not a key![42]

A strong call to the will and to human freedom can be seen in these passages. This other face of modernity, which seemed to be crushed by the rationalization process, comes to the fore as a form of criticism and liberation from totalizing models, from pure instrumental reason, from modernity transformed into an *iron cage,* in which the human being is in fact just one part within a system. However, the question that has always haunted this other pole of modernity is: Where could this ideal of freedom be grounded?

1.2 A Postmodernity?

The discussion around postmodern theories is complex and reaches a large number of areas of knowledge: from physics, to the arts, to philosophy. Many authors have been listed as postmodern: Martin Heidegger, Michael Foucault, Jacques Derrida, Jean-François Ly-

---

40. Fiódor Dostoiévski, *Notas do subsolo* (Porto Alegre: L&PM, 2010), 41.
41. *Ibid.*, 42.
42. *Ibid.*, 42.

otard, Daniel Bell, among others. In order to have a brief overview of postmodernity's most important features I will say a few things about the French philosopher Jean-François Lyotard.

The literary work that gave prominence to Lyotard was published in 1979 under the title *La condition postmoderne* (The Postmodern Condition). Lyotard's main proposition is that the *status* of knowledge is changing. As he himself states in the first chapter of his book:

> Our working hypothesis is that knowledge changes its status at the same time that societies enter the so-called post-industrial age and cultures in the so-called post-modern age.[43]

For him, the notions of truth and progress present in modernity needed to be abandoned. Science, born in the modern era, should not have the *status* of truth, because its legitimacy was within itself, in the *language games* promulgated by itself, being a mere *metanarrative* with its own internal logic.

These metanarratives would be, in fact "[...] great historical-philosophical schemes of progress and perfectibility created by the modern era."[44] Thus, an idea of progress based on these metanarratives would be inconceivable, because there is now an unbelieving attitude toward these meta-narratives, due to the increasing expansion of the notion of relativity in science, in which there is a rejection of the ultimate foundation of truth brought by it.

For this perspective, then, modernity is over. The notion of meaning and progress is criticized and abandoned. For Lyotard, history is not teleological, it does not have a specific purpose. For them, there is no ultimate foundation in explaining reality, all we have are disputing discourses, in a constant power struggle for the one which

---

43. Jean-François Lyotard, *O pós-moderno* (Rio de Janeiro: José Olympio, 1993), 3.
44. Krishan Kumar, *Da sociedade pós-industrial à pós-moderna*, 143.

prevails. In this sense, science, philosophy, the arts, religion, etc., everything is discourse; they are attempts to establish a foundation for the social order.

> All the great narratives of modernity are disregarded, regardless of the field in which they are located: socialism, capitalism, Christianity, romanticism, liberalism, Keynesianism [...], Marxism, and especially all the categories and references of the Enlightenment, such as: dialectic, hermeneutics, emancipation, subject, reason, development, progress, truth, totality, history, equality, freedom, conscience [...].[45]

For this reason, the idea of reason present in modernity would lose its legitimacy as a secure source of truth, because "[...] there are no guarantees that reason will produce liberating consequences,"[46] in the face of the horrors witnessed in the two World Wars. Thus, by delegitimizing the paradigms of modernity, the postmodern theory stands as an explanatory model of contemporary society.

However, as already stated, not all authors agree with the term postmodernity, given that they believe in a process of continuity between modernity and the contemporary, over against the postmodern perspective of rupture and discontinuity. Such is the case of the British sociologist Anthony Giddens, who argues that what we can see today is modernity being radicalized in its existing characteristics.

In the Giddensian explanation, "[...] modern societies have reached a point where they are obliged to reflect on themselves and, at the same time, have developed the capacity to reflect *retrospectively* on themselves."[47] That is, with the increase in the amount and

---

45. Leonildo Pereira de Souza, *O adjetivo e seus substantivos: Uma leitura acerca de elementos do discurso teórico pós-moderno* (Monografia em Ciências Sociais. Pelotas: UFPel, 2003), 53.
46. David Lyon, *Pós-modernidade* (São Paulo: Paulus, 1998), 69.
47. Krishan Kumar, *Da sociedade pós-industrial à pós-moderna*, 152.

speed of information, social institutions and individuals themselves are coerced into living in constant change and transformation. New knowledge emerges all the time, and the old is undermined by the new, creating a need for constant reorganization on the part of the modern societies.

In late modernity, therefore, the *reflexivity* established a *radical doubt* as a standard attitude towards life. Such a process results in an ontological insecurity, being responsible for a widespread *malaise*, caused by the inability to find fixed points, safe harbours of ontological knowledge. Unlike its later stage, classical modernity, through science, still provided these safe havens of knowledge.

Within the Enlightenment project, in the idea of the progress of classical modernity, in fact, it was believed that with the development of science, doubts would gradually diminish as the cosmos was revealed; nature would be scanned and man himself would be understood through the eyes of reason. Nevertheless, "[...] the reflexivity of modernity undermines [even] the certainty of knowledge, even in the central domains of the natural science."[48] What happens, then, is the reverse process: the hypothetical character of scientific knowledge reaches all spheres of human life, making knowledge subject to revision and with a provisional character. As Giddens puts it:

> For when the claims of reason replaced those of tradition, they seemed to offer a sense of certainty greater than that provided by the previous dogma, [however] the reflexivity of modernity does in fact subvert reason, at least where reason is understood as gain of certain knowledge.[49]

In this new context, marked by a great dynamism, the process of identity formation is completely new, one that in pre-modern conditions the formation of individual identity was a process without so

---

48. Anthony Giddens, *Modernidade e identidade*, 26.
49. Anthony Giddens, *As consequências da modernidade*, 46.

many conflicts, since the social environment was more constant, and the reference of tradition was always present. Reflexivity takes identity from a fixed point and throws it into the agitated sea of knowledge that is constantly renewed by a post-traditional society, with an ever-growing diversity of social settings.

It must be pointed out, however, that the terminological discussion concerning the best way to describe the contemporary is quite varied and expresses different theoretical emphases. If Lyotard prefers the term *postmodern,* for the reasons described above, Giddens employs the term *late modern* for pointing out aspects of continuity and radicalization in contrast to the previous period. The Polish sociologist Zygmunt Bauman used the term *liquid modernity,* and the French author Gilles Lipovetsky prefers to use *hypermodernity.*

Such a variety in terminology seems to reveal a very dynamic process that is by no means static. Peter Leithart expresses this idea very clearly when he says that:

> postmodernity is, in sum, a knot of cultural, philosophical, and social developments, arising from intensifications, inversions, and unmasking of modernity, which challenges, doubts and rejects the modern trinity of control, liberation and progress.[50]

1.2.1 Herman Dooyeweerd and Postmodernity

Could Dooyeweerd be framed, then, as a postmodern author once he had profound critiques of modernity? A thorough and deeper answer to this question is not within the horizon of this book. However, it is necessary to address the issue, given its relevance for our context. Dooyeweerd's critique of modernity differs substantially from the postmodern critique. From his perspective, we would still be

---

50. Peter Leithart, *Solomon Among the Postmoderns* (Grand Rapids, Michigan: Brazos Press, 2008), 54.

living the consequences of modernity, in reference to the humanistic ground-motive developed by it, namely, that of *nature and freedom*.

Classical modernity emphasized the pole of nature, with the development of the sciences. Within this context flourished reductionistic ways of seeing the world, such as *mechanicism* in physics, such as with Newton; *organicism* and *evolutionism* in biology as with Spencer and Darwin; and *Positivism* in the social sciences with Augusto Comte. All these *isms* were fruits of the *rationalism* that mechanized, objectified, materialized, and naturalized reality and human existence.

Meanwhile, the period understood as late modernity or postmodernity would have gone to the other extreme of this dualistic relationship, towards the motive of *freedom*. What Dooyeweerd categorized as the personality-ideal was expressed first in the *Romantic* movement. In this pole, there is a strong emphasis on the individual, the subjectivity and personal existence. In one sense, postmodernity would not be in any way an overcoming of modern thought, but an expression, even if in another pole, of it.

Thus, Dooyeweerd does not align himself with the critics of modern reason, in their view that it hinders human freedom. The Dutch author has always suspected autonomous reason alone. For him, the decentralization of reason in (post) modern thought expresses less a rupture, and more a continuous search of the human being for a new idol, within an indissoluble antithesis, resulting from an apostate ground-motive that cannot be strong enough to account for the created order.

Therefore, as we have seen, modernity is not monolithic in its manifestations. So, in what sense is Herman Dooyeweerd's philosophical proposal innovative? How does he construct his critique of modernity? The presentation of Dooyeweerd's intellectual context in dialogue with modernity, as well as the initial outline of his ideas, will be carried out in the following chapter.

2

FROM GENEVA TO AMSTERDAM: DUTCH NEO-CALVINISM AS A RESPONSE TO MODERNITY

IF WE WANT TO HAVE A WIDER VIEW of Herman Doyeweerd's thinking, we need to contextualize it within the framework of neo-Calvinism, a reformation movement in Dutch society that began in the mid-nineteenth century, reaching various spheres of society: from the church to politics, and from philosophy to education. Quite broadly, we can say that this movement, in which its foundations can be found in the Reformed Protestant tradition, developed an update and application of the principles of sixteenth century Calvinism to the Dutch context of the nineteenth and twentieth century.

As discussed in the previous chapter, the changes in various fields of life which originated with modernity reached in full the Dutch society. It is precisely in this scenario that neo-Calvinism developed. In this sense, the humanistic values of the French Revolution, in which its principle of *laïcité* carried strong anti-religious content, were propagated across Europe, forcing the removal of religious values from the public sphere, relegating faith to a private sphere only, in a very hostile attitude toward the Christian faith, specifically.

Allied to the liberal political ideal, the nineteenth century can be thought of as the century of the apex of the belief in human progress through reason. Such rationality needed to be expressed through the modern scientific method, in which its epistemological validity had replaced all other forms of knowing. It is in this context that, for example, the social sciences, such as sociology and anthropology, emerge. Initially, both show serious reservations and even animosity against philosophy, in so far as it would not have scientific value, as expressed by sociologist Augusto Comte's[1] defence of the higher (positive) *scientific state*, in opposition to the less developed earlier stages, such as the *religious* and the *philosophical*. Another example is the ideal of Marx of a *scientific socialism*, as opposed to an *idealistic socialism*.

In this sense, one of the hallmarks of the nineteenth century was the *ideal of science*, articulated in the separation between faith and reason and in the attempt to diminish the influence of Christianity in the areas of public life in Europe, such as culture and politics.

Given that context, the question with which neo-Calvinists were grappling with was: "Could Christianity, after the French Revolution, be revived in such a way as to have a salutary effect in the direction of Western culture?"[2] There was a battle against the modern

---

1. August Comte (1798-1857) was one of the main representatives of the French *Positivism*. He is considered one of the founding fathers of Sociology.
2. L. Kalsbeek, *Contornos da filosofia cristã: a melhor e mais sucinta intro-*

forces of liberalizing Enlightenment. According to Kaslbeeck, "[...] the forces of Roman Catholicism and evangelical Protestantism were too weak to effectively resist the control of *liberal humanism* in the decisive sectors of Dutch culture."[3]

Neo-Calvinism is articulated, among other reasons, as a response to these challenges generated by modernity. This movement had its main exponent in the figure of Abraham Kuyper (1837-1920). However, names like Guillaume Groen Van Prinsterer (1801-1876), Herman Bavinck (1854-1921) – admittedly, its systematic theologian – and Dirk Vollenhoven (1892-1978), Dooyeweerd›s brother-in-law, were also part of the movement in its early days.[4]

Commenting on the importance of Dooyeweerd to the development of the neo-Calvinist tradition, the Brazilian philosopher Ricardo Quadros Gouvêa says:

> [...] without Dooyeweerd there would be no reformational philosophy, and the fragmentation of the other thinkers cited would be inevitable. Dooyeweerd developed a philosophy that historically served as the unifying pole of the philosophical thought of people engaged in the Reformed or Calvinist tradition.[5]

Having said that, Abraham Kuyper was still its most known representative. Kuyper was a journalist, politician, pastor, founder of a political party (*anti-revolutionary party*), Prime Minister of the

---

dução à filosofia reformada de Herman Dooyeweerd (São Paulo: Cultura Cristã, 2015), 15.
3. *Ibid.* 2015, 15.
4. Cf. Rodomar Ramlow, *O neocalvinismo holandês: Temas e autores* (Anais do Congresso Internacional de Teologia. São Leopoldo: EST, 2012, v. 1, p. 1701-1716), 1702.
5. Ricardo Quadros Gouvêa, *O lado bom do calvinismo: ensaios acerca de um calvinismo saudável* (São Paulo: Fonte Editorial, 2013), 222.

Netherlands (1901-1905) and founder of the renowned Vrije Universiteit Amsterdam (Free University of Amsterdam).[6] In one of his most celebrated works *Lectures on Calvinism*, best known as the *Stone Lectures* (1898) delivered in Princeton, USA, he asserts:

> There is no doubt, then, that Christianity is exposed to great and serious dangers. Two *life systems* are in mortal combat. Modernism is committed to building its own world from elements of natural man and to build man himself from elements of nature.[7]

The question that needed to be answered, according to neo-Calvinists, was how to make Christian influence public. "Kuyper's goal has been described as the 're-Christianization' of Dutch culture [...]."[8] For Jonathan Chaplin, "[...] Kuyperian neo-Calvinism can thus be classified as a modernizing and progressive form of democratic pluralism, inspired by a traditional religious perspective [...]."[9]

In a sense, neo-Calvinism can be comprehended as a Christian response to the dominant secular values of that context, without, however, being a de-legitimization of the cultural, political and economic spheres – as if they were problematic in themselves, but seeing them as creational structures, defending their constant reformation from a Christian perspective. As a practical example of this response, Kuyper founded in 1879, as mentioned before, the anti-revolutionary party (*Anti-Revolutionaire Partij*, ARP). The central motto was the reform of social structures as opposed to the idea of a radical revolution. Commenting on Kuyper and his influence on

---

6. For Kuyper, the idea of a *free* university was connected to a freedom in relationship both to the State as well as to the church.
7. Abraham Kuyper, *Calvinismo* (São Paulo: Cultura Cristã, 2003), 19.
8. Jonathan Chaplin, *Herman Dooyeweerd: Christian philosopher of State and Civil Society* (Indiana: Notre Dame, 2011), 21.
9. *Ibid.*, 22.

politics, Chaplin states:

> Kuyper was an early advocate for universal adult (male) suffrage. The party was formed in a breach with the aristocratic conservative movement with which the "anti-revolutionaries" had initially been allied. It was not only the first Christian Democratic party to be established in Europe, but the first mass political party, period. Just as original Calvinism inspired democratizing movements in the seventeenth century, so Dutch neo-Calvinism under Kuyper's leadership did in the nineteenth.[10]

The main theme addressed by neo-Calvinism was the unity of creation and redemption, of nature and grace. Similarly, there was an affirmation of Christianity as a system of life, with particular emphasis on creational law and sphere sovereignty, which would influence the name of the philosophical tradition of Dooyeweerd: *Cosmonomic Philosophy* or *Philosophy of the Law-Idea* (*De Wijsbegeerte der Wetsidee* in Dutch) – mainly known as Reformational Philosophy.

Another element highlighted by this movement was the postulate of the French reformer John Calvin on the theological meaning of the *Fall*. Following the Genevan theologian, Kuyper defended the doctrine of humanity's total fall in sin, being a strong opponent of the idea of a Thomistic *natural reason*, whose emphasis was on the possibility of a human knowledge of God from rational structures not affected by sin – a *natural theology*. For Kuyper, all areas of life were affected by sin, including rational capacity, hence the need for reformation of the mind.

In this sense, a philosophy that would have as its starting point man's autonomous reason *per se* would disregard a central

---

10. Jonathan Chaplin, *The Full Weight of our Convictions: The Point of Kuyperian Pluralism*. [S.l] 01 nov. 2013. Disponível em: <https://www.cardus.ca/comment/article/4069/the-point-of-kuyperian-pluralism/>.

aspect of human anthropology: the presence of sin. For this reason, with this theological foundation, the project of a Christian philosophy would have its space, differentiating itself, however, from *scholasticism*.

Upon the foundation of neo-Calvinism and Dooyeweerd's reformational philosophy, this tradition of thought continued to develop and is echoed these days by different authors, institutions, and academic associations.

Some study and research centres are important for the organization and contact of those who work within the framework of the Kuyperian-Dooyeweerdian tradition. A few contemporary ones worth mentioning are: the *Abraham Kuyper Center for Science and Religion*, located at the Free University of Amsterdam, in the Netherlands; the *Abraham Kuyper Center for Public Theology*, based in the Princeton Theological Seminary, USA; and the *Association for Reformational Philosophy*, also based in the Netherlands. This association was formed by Dooyeweerd and Vollenhoven in 1935, under the name of the *Association for Calvinistic Philosophy*. Currently, the Association has more than 500 members around the world, maintaining the academic journal *Philosophia Reformata* and promoting events and publications from, and in dialogue with, the neo-Calvinist tradition.

It is important to note that the use of the term reformational philosophy is intended to identify the Amsterdam tradition. Until 1955 the *Association for Reformational Philosophy* was called *Association for Calvinistic Philosophy*. However, due to the perception of the ecumenical scope and the comprehensive nature of this philosophy, the term *reformational* began to be employed, as the project took a dimension of being a Christian philosophy.[11]

---

11. Cf. Jonathan Chaplin, 2011, 30.

2.1 The Reform of Theoretical Thinking

Under the influence of the Dutch neo-Calvinist movement, Dooyeweerd believed that theoretical thought itself needed to be reformed and critiqued from the Christian ground-motive of *creation-fall-redemption*, in which a more detailed foundation can be found both in the *Institutes* of John Calvin and in the systematic theology of Herman Bavinck. For the Dutch philosopher, following the Genevan reformer, a philosophical *insight* into the structure of reality would only be possible with the knowledge of *who* the human person is, and such knowledge is inseparable from the knowledge of God.[12]

What seems to be at stake in the Dooyeweerdian philosophical work is precisely this affirmation of the religious nature of man, which would always act as a presupposition in any intellectual endeavour, be it philosophical or scientific. This presupposition cannot become the object of any area of knowledge, since it is from it – whose nature is supratemporal – that reality that is interpreted in the horizon of time.

For Ricardo Quadros Gouvêa: "[the] introduction of religion is not, therefore, an option for the philosopher, but a choice based on facts, a necessary and inevitable choice, which happens in the thinking of all, Christians or non-Christians, believers or unbelievers."[13] In this manner, "[...] when we try to think theoretically, our view of the totality will be present as a 'tacit dictionary of presuppositions'."[14] This is always pre-theoretical, taking place within our experience of

---

12. Cf. Herman Dooyeweerd, *A New Critique of Theoretical Thought*, 9.
13. Ricardo Quadros Gouvêa, *O lado bom do calvinismo*, 274-75.
14. Guilherme Carvalho, "Sociedade, justiça e política na filosofia de cosmovisão cristã: uma introdução ao pensamento social de Herman Dooyeweerd." In: Maurício Cunha et al. (Org.), *Cosmovisão cristã e transformação: espiritualidade, razão e ordem social* (Viçosa, MG: Ultimato, 2006, p. 189-218), 192.

the world[15], not being subject to objectification, which differs profoundly from a Greek conception of philosophy, which sees reason as a focal opening point of reality itself compared to our ordinary experience.

Regarding the project of a Christian philosophy, Kalsbeek states:

> [...] the most important premise of this philosophy is in its assumption that reality is created by a God whose will is the sovereign and redemptive law to reality. [And yet], Dooyeweerd did not just argue that a *Christian* philosophy is religiously founded; he claims that *all* philosophical and scientific efforts are determined by underlying religious motives.[16]

The *Philosophy of the Law-Idea*, the original title of Dooyeweerd's main work, was translated into English under his supervision as *A New Critique of Theoretical Thought*, in reference to the fundamental works of modern philosophical thought: the *critical* works of Immanuel Kant, especially his *Critique of Pure Reason*. This is an indicative of the Dooyeweerdian enterprise: re-thinking the epistemological foundations of philosophy from the critique of the autonomy of reason as a valid foundation for the philosophical endeavour as proposed by Kant.

In his analysis, Dooyeweerd rethinks the structure of knowledge itself, asserting that theoretical thinking constitutes an antithetical relationship that does not correspond to reality. In one of his lectures, he states:

> [the] distance between the logical aspect of our thinking and the non- logical aspect of our field of study [...] produces an antithetical

---

15. In here, we can see a profound influence of Marin Heidegger's *Being and Time* (1927) on Dooyeweerd's thinking, as admitted by himself in the preface of the NC.
16. L. Kalsbeek, 2015, 28.

relation, in which the logical aspect of our thought is opposed to the non-logical aspect of the reality investigated [...]. From this theoretical antithesis the scientific problem arises.[17]

In this way, philosophy could not choose one of the terms of this antithetical relationship as a starting point in investigating the structure of reality. For the Dutch author, it would be impossible to establish as a starting point – in the manner of Kant – a dialectical opposition between reason (logical aspect) and reality, our common experience, for a fundamental reason: this opposition is a *purely theoretical abstraction*. According to Dooyeweerd, the only antithesis in reality is the *religious antithesis*. Thus, he directs his criticisms to the idea of a dialectic that dissolves any idea or absolute value, which constitutes a criticism of one of the main elements of Western philosophy, in which its heritage is Greek.

Philosophy and any other theoretical endeavour must seek its starting point in the supratemporal order. It would make no sense to identify in the dialectic relationship an absolute, given that it is relative. Philosophy is theoretical, and in its constitution it remains bound to the relativity of all human thought. As such, philosophy itself needs an absolute starting point.[18] To do otherwise would be an absolutization of a finite aspect or a *reductionism*.

This is a key point in the Dooyeweerdian philosophical system: the absolute exists only in the religious. Such an absolute is an indissoluble antithesis, which cannot be synthesized with any other form of thought. The only division introduced in reality was the one that came with (original) sin. In this fallen condition, the human being is

---

17. Herman Dooyeweerd, *Introduction to a Transcendental Criticism of Philosophic Thought*. Available in: <http://www.reformationalpublishingproject.com/pdf_books/Scanned_Books_PDF/IntroductiontoaTranscendentalCriticismofPhilosophicThought.pdf>.

18. Herman Dooyeweerd, *Roots of Western Culture*, Paideia Press, 2012, 8.

alienated from God, from himself and from creation.

For Dooyeweerd, an absolute is also called a *religious ground-motive*, which controls and regulates the theoretical, social, political, and cultural developments of a human group. According to him, in the case of the West, there are four religious ground-motives that have predominated throughout history: the Greek dualism *form and matter*, the scholastic *nature and grace*, the humanistic *nature and freedom*, and the biblical motive *creation-fall-redemption*.

2.2 A Biblical View of the Heart and the Development of a Critical Philosophy

The philosophical project developed by Dooyeweerd can also be called a critical philosophy, as is the case with Kant's, given that it seeks to understand the starting point of knowledge, subjecting it to a rigorous examination. Besides this, his philosophy can also be called a *transcendental philosophy*, as it pursues a *concentration point* or a supratemporal *Archimedean point*, capable of analyzing the theoretical attitude of thought.

At the beginning of one of his transcribed lectures, *Introduction to the Transcendental Criticism of Philosophic Thought*, the Dutch author questions the Kantian thesis of identifying *reason* as the starting point for theoretical thinking, as an autonomous and independent element. Theoretical thinking as well as scientific thinking would have deeper roots. Commenting on Kantian philosophy, he says that:

> He did not examine the possibility of a critical theory of human knowledge as a purely scientific theory. He invites his readers, in the introduction to his celebrated work The Critique *of Pure Reason*, to accept no other datum than Pure Reason. Consequently, the theoretical attitude of thought has for him nothing problematic.[19]

---

19. Herman Dooyeweerd, *Introduction to a Transcendental Criticism of Philosophic Thought*. Available in: <http://www.reformationalpublish-

Therefore, he criticizes the transcendence given to theoretical thinking in Kant's vision, suggesting that the logical aspect of experience cannot be elevated to the status of a starting point for theoretical knowledge. For Dooyeweerd, the starting point, the *archimedean point*, is found in the biblical concept of the *heart*, the transcendental aspect of the human being, which cannot be reduced to one of the aspects of reality. The heart can also be understood as the *human ego*, which is defined as "[...] the central seat of *the imago Dei*."[20]

The heart should not be confused with the modern association of it as being emotions and feelings alone. In the Judaeo-Christian understanding the heart represents the ultimate orientation and direction that the whole person is taking. It stores deep desires and aspirations, it represents who we are as a unity, as beings created in the image and likeness of a God that cannot be reduced to any of His attributes. So, the heart speaks of that which is irreducible in us as well.

The human heart is necessarily oriented in one direction or another: either towards the Creator or towards creation, either towards God or towards idols. In this sense, Guilherme de Carvalho observes that:

> When the ego rejects the relationship with the personal and transcendental God, the true origin, it is obliged to seek another source of meaning, absolutizing particular aspects of its experience and giving different directions – always immanent – to its structural religious impulse.[21]

---

ingproject.com/pdf_books/Scanned_Books_PDF/Introductiontoa-TranscendentalCriticismofPhilosophicThought.pdf>.
20. Herman Dooyeweerd, *No crepúsculo do pensamento ocidental*, 167.
21. Guilherme de Carvalho, "Herman Dooyeweerd, reformador da razão." In: Herman Dooyeweerd, *No crepúsculo do pensamento* (São Paulo: Edi-

In fact, this orientation of the heart is connected to a human need to search for their *origin* (*arche* in Greek) or for a *non-dependent reality*,[22] term used by the philosopher Roy Clouser. It follows from this observation that, even before the theoretical attitude of thought, there is a presupposition of origin, an attribution to something or someone as a non-dependent reality, by which and in which the ultimate meaning is realized. From this principle comes Dooyeweerd's criticism of the supposed religious neutrality of thought, as there would be no philosophy with a neutral starting point.

Based on Dooyeweerdian philosophy, Roy Clouser states that:

> [a] religious belief always functions as a *regulative presupposition* to any abstract theory, and that this is unavoidable not merely owing to the historical/social presence of such beliefs in our culture but because it arises out of the very process of theory making itself.[23]

In other words, religious belief cannot be isolated from the process of theoretical construction. It would function, according to this perspective, as a regulatory assumption for any theoretical endeavour. From this point of view, the modern separation between faith and reason, and the autonomy of the latter, would make no sense. For Carvalho,

> [Dooyeweerd] takes up the Greek, Cartesian and Kantian question about the nature of the *cogito*. Who is the self that thinks? [...] the critical examination of the *thinking self* reveals that it does not have an essential content in itself [...], it seeks it outside of itself, in a source that

---

tora Hagnos, 2010), 30.
22. Roy A. Clouser, *The Myth of Religious Neutrality:* An essay on the hidden role of religious belief in theories, University of Notre Dame Press, 2005, 3.
23. *Ibid.*, 3.

is able to account for the diversity of its experience.[24]

Therefore, for reformational philosophy, the Socratic "know yourself", as in Augustine and Calvin, is by nature religious, because the knowledge of God and of oneself go together. The condition of any philosophical endeavour is the knowledge of the religious presuppositions present in the heart, which is either directed to the Creator or to an element of the created order.

2.2.1 A Private Belief?

It must be pointed out, therefore, that at the same time that modernity was built on the basis of religion, and in dialogue with it, modernity also attempted to separate the religious and rational dimensions of the human being, developing a project of human autonomy upon the foundation of autonomous reason, which could be more accurately described as a form of *rationalism*, a reduction of everything to the *rational* aspect of reality. It relegated belief to a private sphere, defending the ideal of a neutral reason as the only means through which one could engage in the public square. As Dooyeweerd pointed out, this view of a religiously neutral rationality, still found grounds for its development in various fields in his own time. And I would add that it does so even today in the early 21st century.

In this sense, the study and reflection of Dooyeweerd's critique could be a powerful analytical instrument, in which its content is the exposition of a dogmatic belief, arising with modernity – of the privatization of faith – based on the belief of the religious autonomy of reason. His Christian philosophical critique allows us to broaden the theoretical horizon to understand the complex reality that we inhabit.

---

24. Guilherme de Carvalho, "Herman Dooyeweerd, reformador da razão." In: Herman Dooyeweerd, *No crepúsculo do pensamento*, 30.

In addition, the studying and the exploration of the philosophy developed by the Dutch author finds an echo today regarding the great themes present in our societies: the relationship and points of contact between faith and reason, the place of religion in contemporary societies, the conversation between religion and science and, consequently, the role of theology in dialogue with other areas of knowledge, etc.

Therefore, after reflecting on the general characteristics of modernity, as well as a succinct presentation of the Dutch author's intellectual context and critical perspective, it is now time to have a closer look at Herman Dooyeweerd›s philosophical program and his cosmonomic project. What are the elements that make it up? How does he connect philosophy and Christianity? What are the concepts used to build his philosophical system? Further explorations into his ideas is the aim of the next chapter.

3

WHAT HAS AMSTERDAM TO DO WITH ATHENS?

The Development of a Christian Philosophy

3.1 Philosophy and Christianity

AT FIRST, THE MENTION of the term *Christian philosophy* might take us back, exclusively, to the medieval period, more precisely to medieval *scholasticism*. The question *What has Athens to do with Jerusalem?*[1] has always been an issue for Christianity. After all, what is the relationship between the belief system of Christianity and the very nature of philosophy? Is a Christian philosophy even possible? What would the implication be?

The main debates about the relationship between philosophy

---

1. Tertuliano, *De praescriptione haereticorum*, c. 7.

and the Christian faith are normally associated with a conversation or conflict between *philosophy* and *theology*,[2] which in Dooyeweerd cannot be taken as the same, in as much as theology – as a *special science* – would not have privileged access to the truth. In this sense, the cosmological thinker does not intend to subordinate philosophy to theology, as if theology were the true philosophy.

The tension between philosophy and Christianity has been present since the beginning of the development of Christianity. We have an indication of this encounter – or clash – of worldviews from the very life of Jesus, since the Empire that dominated the region of Palestine was the Roman Empire, which, at the time, was under strong Hellenic cultural influence. Furthermore , the biblical narrative describes the apostle of the Gentiles, the Pharisee converted to Christianity[3], Paul of Tarsis – one of the greatest propagators of Christianity in the first century outside the Jewish context – as someone who had significant encounters with Greek philosophers.[4]

This relationship between Christianity and philosophy becomes more explicit after the advance and institutionalization of Christianity in the first centuries. In this context, the Bishop of Hippo, Augustine (354-430 AD) articulated a reinterpretation of Platonism from a Christian perspective, developing a synthesis between the two systems, what has been known as a Christianization of Plato or a Platonization of Christianity. Another notable Christian who, in the High Middle Ages, fostered dialogue – and a synthesis – between Christian faith and Aristotle's philosophical thought was Thomas Aquinas (1225-1274).

Furthermore, even though I am aware of the richness of the Pa-

---

2. Wolfhart Pannenberg, *Filosofia e teologia* (São Paulo: Paulinas, 2008), 17.
3. See Acts 9.1-19.
4. See Acts 17.16-34.

tristic tradition of the Church Fathers – from Tertullian to Gregory of Nyssa – I will not dwell on the analysis of this period for reasons of the objective and scope of this work. It is important to note, however, that Christianity and philosophy have a long tradition of dialogue, at times conciliatory, at times conflictual. In one way or another, however, excluding this period in the study of philosophy would at least be a very serious fault. In this chapter, I will address Dooyeweerd's response to the question of Tertullian – What has Jerusalem to do with Athens? In it, the main elements present in his philosophical system will be explored, as well as the conceptual language present in the work of the Dutch philosopher.

The chapter is structured thus: it begins by explaining the meaning of *cosmonomic*, as I address the concept of *Sphere-Sovereignty* created by Abraham Kuyper, and developed by Dooyeweerd as a *Modal Ontology*. Right after that, I reflect on the Dooyeweerdian *anthropology* and, finally, I present his perspective regarding the relationship between *philosophy* and *theology*.

3.1.1 The Structure of Reality: Cosmonomic Modal Ontology

Starting from the idea that the role of philosophy is to understand and discern the structure of reality, the relationship between the whole and its parts, that is, its different dimensions – Dooyeweerd defends a de-*essentialization* of the *cosmos* as an initial starting point for understanding reality, since no dimension of it can become the foundation of knowledge. It is important to emphasize that his understanding is that knowledge takes place in the order of time, since "[...] we cannot philosophize about what transcends this temporality [...]"[5],because what is supratemporal is absolute, therefore, antithetically indissoluble.

---

5. K. J. Popma, *Inleiding in de Wijsbeerte* (Kampen, 1956), 94. Apud: L. Kalsbeek, *Contornos da filosofia cristã*, 31.

A *cosmonomical* proposal points to a cosmic order, whose meaning – order and/or law – is a gift. In other words, the foundation of the *cosmos* is outside of it, in the Creator. For this reason, the Dutch philosopher claims that the Creator God is the *arché* or the *origin* of the human search for the meaning of the whole.⁶ "An overview of the whole is not apart of our view of the origin, or the ἀρχή [...]."⁷

> This would be nothing less than an unrestricted admission of *Christian theism* as an idea of cosmic order and origin; not of theism in the Aristotelian-Thomistic sense, properly speaking, but in the Calvinist sense: [...] sovereign God, principle of the cosmic order, beyond all law – but upholder of all laws, transcendent and distinct from all creatures, and from all spheres of our temporal experience.⁸

The natural impulse of the human being would be to orientate the *heart* – understood in Dooyeweerd as the human religious centre, from the Hebrew conception of heart – to an absolute, insofar as this is the law of the cosmos, hence the concept of the *cosmonomic*.

The soil on which Dooyeweerd would later develop his systematic philosophy or, more precisely, his *ontology of modes of experience* or *modal ontology*, was the idea of *sovereignty-spheres* developed by Abraham Kuyper. As already mentioned here, the neo-Calvinist effort was to maintain the influence and relevance of Christianity in public terms. For that, the notion of *sovereignty* – and the legitimacy of power – needed to be reformed. According to Kuyper and his followers, sovereignty could not be based on the modern idea of the *social contract* – be it after the manner of Hobbes, Locke or Rousseau.

---

6. Herman Dooyeweerd, *A New Critique of Theoretical Thought*, 8.
7. *Ibid.*, 8.
8. Guilherme Carvalho, "Sociedade, justiça e política na filosofia de cosmovisão cristã." In: Maurício Cunha et al. (Org.), *Cosmovisão cristã e transformação*, p. 195.

A *contractualist* model of legitimacy of sovereignty was, according to Kuyper, the supreme expression, in political terms, of human autonomy in relation to God, which had been developed in the modern period.[9] This expression would have its roots in a religious motive. This autonomy was expressed in Hobbes, for example, when he argues that the modern state receives its sovereignty from the pact made by individuals, who, in exchange for security, surrender their freedom to the *Leviathan* (the State), which now has the power over other spheres of life.

From a Kuyperian understanding, however, it is not individual rights or the modern State – as an essentialized entity – that found and legitimized power. From a Christian perspective, they argued, there is only one sovereign: God Himself. A first statement that is made, therefore, in relation to the State, is the following: the State cannot be God.

Likewise, opposing an ideal of freedom founded on the absence of norms and with an emphasis on human freedom, Guilherme de Carvalho deals with the mission of the Christian and the church in the world when he affirms:

> There are those who think it would be good [...] to adopt a [...] libertarian version of divinity, as if by expanding the field of human initiative, Christians would become less passive [...]. If we become more missional, more active and more responsible just because we have an elevated sense of our human autonomy, of our powers of intervention, of our ability to break through historical dominations, I ask: whose glory will it be?[10]

---

9. See Abraham Kuyper, *Calvinismo*, 54.
10. Guilherme de Carvalho, *A objeção reformada ao dogma da autonomia religiosa da razão*. Revista Diálogo e Antítese, vol. 1, nº 1, 2009, pp. 4-53, p. 43.

Thus, there would be no contradiction, from the Kuyperian-Dooyeweerdian tradition, between the sovereignty and the power of God and human freedom, which is to say that the law does not contradict grace, but rather is in harmony with it, given that the law is the condition of human freedom, not a barrier to it.

Based on this premise, Kuyper outlines the idea that different spheres of life have their own sovereignty, supported by the *creational law* and *historically differentiated*. In this sense, the State would still have its sovereignty – restricted, however, to its area of operation, namely, to the promotion of justice. However, the family, the economy, the church (or other religious denominations), education, the arts and so on, would all have their own foundation, in which their origin, it is important to reaffirm, is not in the social contract. Rather, they would be relatively autonomous spheres in relation to the others. With this, the neo-Calvinists wanted, among other things, to limit State interference in the different aspects of life. As Kuyper himself states:

> In this independent character is necessarily involved a special higher authority, that is intentionally called *sovereignty in the individual social spheres,* so that may be clear that these different developments of social life *have nothing above them except God,* and that the State cannot interfere here and has nothing to order in its field.[11]

While this neo-Calvinist project, drafted by Abraham Kuyper, concerned a theological elaboration, with sociological and political implications, regarding the interface between Church, State, and social institutions, the efforts of Herman Dooyeweerd were principally to develop from this initial scheme a more comprehensive theory, with an ontological character, in which its articulation would serve as a foundation for further developments in different fields of

---

11. Abraham Kuyper, *Calvinismo,* 98.

knowledge. It was under this influence that Dooyeweerd developed his *modal ontology*.

3.2 Modal Ontology

In moving from a sociological approach to a philosophical one, Dooyeweerd uses the concepts of *modal aspects* or *modalities of experience*,[12] to refer to the different ways – *the how* – by which human beings experience reality. For the Amsterdam philosopher, the pre-theoretical, everyday human experience is not divided, rather, it is integral and unbreakable. However, from the theoretical attitude of thought, it is possible to discern the different aspects that compose this experience.

The illustration he uses to explain this system assumes that reality is *meaning*, given as a gift from the Creator. This meaning is like the sunlight refracted through a prism, scattering into different colours and nuances, but coming from the same source. As he puts it:

> This whole diversity of modal aspects of our experience makes sense only within the order of time. It refers to a supra-temporal, central unity and fullness of meaning in our experiential world.[13]

Humans experience this meaning in *different modes*, without qualitatively differentiating them before theoretical abstraction. "For each aspect, particular *laws* or *norms* are found."[14] This analogy explains how Christ's sovereignty is expressed in the world. God has a single will, perfect and consistent. However, when his will "crosses" the prism of time, it is expressed in different laws. Each law, in the creation of God, can be compared to one of the colours of the spec-

---

12. Cf. Herman Dooyeweerd, *In the Twilight of Western Thought*, Paideia Press, 2012, 7.
13. *Ibid.*, 8.
14. L. Kalsbeek, *Contornos da filosofia cristã*, 38.

trum of light.[15]

For Dooyeweerd, however, these aspects do not find their basis in each other – they are not mere *epiphenomena* – and cannot be reduced to each other, constituting what he called the *irreducibility of the aspects*.[16] That is a parallel with Kuyper's idea of the *sovereignty of the spheres*. These aspects would be the expression of the order of time itself, which finds meaning in their coherence.

It is important to note, however, that these *aspects* of reality are not equivalent to concrete events in reality:

> These aspects do not, as such, refer to a concrete what, i.e., to concrete things or events, but only to the how, i.e., the particular and fundamental mode, or manner, in which we experience them. [...] They should not be identified with the concrete phenomena of empirical reality, which function, in principle, in all of these aspects.[17]

As an aspect discernible by the process of theoretical abstraction of thought, these aspects are completely malleable. Once they are proven to be reduced to another aspect, they lose their character of *irreducibility*.

The 15 modal aspects suggested by Dooyeweerd that comprise his modal ontology are:

---

15. Guilherme de Carvalho, "O senhorio de Cristo e a missão da igreja na cultura: a ideia de soberania e sua aplicação." In: Leonardo Ramos et al. (Org.), *Fé cristã e cultura contemporânea* (Viçosa, MG: Ultimato, 2009), 78.
16. See Herman Dooyeweerd, *A New Critique of Theoretical Thought*, 3.
17. Herman Dooyeweerd, *In the Twilight of Western Thought*, Collected Works, Series B – Volume 16, Paideia Press, 2012, 7.

	Modal Aspect	Field of Study
1	Numerical	Mathematics
2	Spatial	Spatial Geometry
3	Kinematical	Kinematics
4	Physical	Physics/Chemistry
5	Biotic	Biology
6	Sensorial (Emotional)	Psychology
7	Logical	Logic
8	Historical	History
9	Linguistical	Linguistics/Semiotics
10	Social	Sociology
11	Economical	Economics
12	Aesthetical	Art/Design/Architecture
13	Judicial	Law
14	Ethical	Ethics
15	Pistic (Faith)	Theology

None of these *modes of experience* could be reduced to each other, as I said before. For example, a theory that seeks to explain the meaning of *the pistic aspect* (relative to faith) in terms of *the historical aspect* would be committing a *reductionism*. Such reductionism could only be identified to the extent that the view of the whole – a view that is religious – of this theory were to be identified, in which its assumption would be based on the absolutization of one aspect of reality.

This order of the aspects (spheres) is not random. According to Carvalho,

> The posterior spheres would be "founded" in the previous ones, without being merely derived phenomena (*epiphenomena*) in relation to

them. And each sphere would "mirror" the totality of *the* cosmic *meaning*, mirroring that can be described by anticipatory and retrocipatory *analogies* [...]. An example: in the expression "economy of thought", we have an anticipatory analogy of the economic sphere within the logical sphere.[18]

These modal aspects, therefore, represent their conception of reality and the way in which the human being experiences it. However, all these modal aspects in their coherence cannot define *who* the human person is. All of them point to a central dimension: the *ego* or the *heart*, which would transcend the temporal order, pointing to its Giver. It is important to note that, as a theory, these aspects are categorizations and not immutable structures of reality.

3.2.1 Who is the I? Dooyeweerd's Anthropology

In the foundations of modern science, a fundamental paradigm is embedded in the structure of scientific knowledge: the relationship between a *subject* (knowing) and an *object* (knowable). One of the questions Dooyeweerd wants to answer is who this subject is. After all, who *is* the human person in essence? *Is* there such an essence? What characterizes the human in its centrality? Who is the *I* that thinks, the knowing subject?

Modern philosophy, since Descartes, has been working on this issue – the nature of the *cogito (I think)*. After all, what defines the human person: a moral, rational, political being? In addition, with the advent of the sciences that emerged with modernity, such as biology and later cultural anthropology, new questions about the human nature were brought to the fore.

From the biological sciences and new discoveries, such as the hu-

---

18. Guilherme Carvalho, "Sociedade, justiça e política na filosofia de cosmovisão cristã." In: Maurício Cunha et al. (Org.), *Cosmovisão cristã e transformação*, p. 196.

man genetic structure, some questions arise: Would humans not be a mere product of impersonal forces, whose definition could be reduced to the physical-chemical structures that keep the biological structure alive in a struggle for survival? Using the Marxist analogy of base and superstructure, some biologists have asserted that certain dimensions of human life, such as *morality* and *faith*, for example, would be superstructures – derived, therefore, from the biological base, the basis of which would be selfishness, insofar as survival would be the ultimate goal for human life.[19]

On the other hand, the American anthropologist Clifford Geertz, in the essay *The Impact of the Concept of Culture on the Concept of Man*,[20] argues that, before we speak of human nature, we would need to define man as an animal that operates at the symbolic level and that seeks its references in a system of symbols that is culture. In the face of cultural diversity, according to Geertz, it would be thoughtless to think of a universal human being without first thinking about the particularities of his cultural background. If, on the one hand, cultural anthropology "protects" the human against a reduction to the biotic aspect, on the other, does it not itself take the risk of reducing it to culture?

The Dooyeweerdian anthropological perspective begins with the statement that the human *ego*, the centre of life, in which its biblical correspondence would be the idea of the *heart*, cannot be defined by any of the modal aspects of reality. Such an assertion is made from the idea that the modes of experience belong to time. To identify, therefore, the human being with some of these modalities, would be to reduce us to what we are not – in the sense that we are not (only) that. In this way, perspectives that reduce human anthropology to the biotic aspect or to culture, would be classified by Dooyeweerd as

---

19. See Richard Dawkins, *The Selfish Gene*, Oxford University Press, 2016.
20. See Clifford Geertz, *The Interpretation of Cultures*, Fontana Press, 1993.

reductionism: In these cases, a *biologism* and a *culturalism*.

His understanding of who we are as humans appears when he asserts: "The central unit of the selfhood is not to be found in the modal diversity of the temporal order. A physico—psychical I does not exist, neither a logical, a historical, nor a moral self"[21]. In the same way, the relationship *I-Thou* cannot be the source provider of meaning to human experience as it is also in the order of time. The solution, according to the Dutch philosopher, is to think of the human *ego* from its religious relationship with its origin: the *arché*.[22] The *self*, therefore, finds meaning in God, the giver of its image.

The Dooyeweerdian person is religious by nature. It is worth mentioning, however, that this idea, present in Calvin, of an innate religious impulse is closer to a *sensus divinitas* than to the Thomistic idea of a *sensus Dei*.[23] The heart, the religious centre, is not, as in Thomas Aquinas, naturally oriented towards the true God. Rather, under the influence of the fall, this impulse can be channelled in any direction.

For the Brazilian philosopher Gouvêa,

> [...] what Dooyeweerd wanted to prove, and believes he has proved, is that the rationalist dogmatism of modern philosophy that claims autonomy and supremacy for human reason is not a religiously neutral conviction, but depends on a supratheoretical religious understanding, a consequence of an existential religious positioning of the subject himself, even though this attitude rejects this classification and even though this attitude leads the subject to deny its own existence.[24]

---

21. Herman Dooyeweerd, *In the Twilight of Western Thought*, Collected Works, Series B – Volume 16, Paideia Press, 2012, 21.
22. Herman Dooyeweerd, *A New Critique of Theoretical Thought*, 8.
23. Guilherme de Carvalho, In: Herman Dooyeweerd, *No crepúsculo do pensamento*, 82. Nota de rodapé 75.
24. Ricardo Quadros Gouvêa, *O lado bom do calvinismo*, 280.

WHAT HAS AMSTERDAM TO DO WITH ATHENS?

In this sense, we could make a connection between the concept of *religion* in Dooyeweerd and in the German theologian Paul Tillich. The concept of orienting the heart to an absolute religious origin is close to the idea of *unconditioned* or *ultimate concern*, presented by Tillich.[25] As much as there are profound differences between them in what concerns the content of this ultimate concern and of what and who this origin is, the idea is similar: Every human being is religious and somehow attributes absolute value to something or to somebody.

Following the Dooyeweerdian tradition, Roy Clouser says "[that] "A religious belief is a belief in something as divine per se no matter how that is further described, where 'divine per se' means having unconditionally non-dependent reality."[26]

In view of these statements, Dooyeweerd's effort, in his anthropology, is to affirm the multiplicity of the composition of human experience and existence. In this direction, his project is very close to the criticism made by the *existentialists* to the rationalism of modernity. For Dooyeweerd, the human ego remains a "mystery." Trying, therefore, to fully capture the ego would be impossible:

> The mystery of the human I is that it is, indeed, nothing in itself; that is to say, it is nothing as long as we try to conceive it apart from the three central relations which alone give it meaning. First, our human ego is related to our whole temporal existence[...]. Second, it finds himself, indeed, in an essential communal relation to the egos of his fellowmen. Third, it points beyond itself to its central relation to its divine Origin in Whose image man was created.[27]

---

25. Guilherme de Carvalho, *A objeção reformada ao dogma da autonomia religiosa da razão*, 9.
26. Roy A. Clouser, 2005, 23.
27. *Herman Dooyeweerd, In the Twilight of Western Thought,* Collected

Therefore, the understanding of who the human being is requires knowledge of the relationship that the human being establishes with his divine origin. Dooyeweerd points to a self-knowledge that is only possible through the true God, whose revelation is found in Jesus Christ. Furthermore, since reality presents itself as different modes to human beings, "[...] an intermodal synthesis can only be carried out by something that does not originate in theoretical thinking [...], since it is in the I that the synthesis of pre-theoretical ordinary experience is verified [...]."[28]

For the Dutch philosopher, there is a deep misunderstanding in the dualistic and synthetic anthropological conceptions. The conceptions that divide the human being between a material and an immaterial dimension – soul – being connected by a substance, tend, according to Dooyeweerd, to postulate that the main human characteristic, functioning as the frontier between nature and ethics, between human and animal, is the rational function, the essence of which would even resist death.

> This view of man was, indeed, taken from Greek philosophy, which sought the center of our human existence in reason, that is, in the intellect. But in this entire image of man there was no room for the real – that is, the religious center of our existence, which in the Holy Scripture is called our heart, the spiritual root of all the temporal manifestations of our life.[29]

The way to escape from synthetic-dualistic anthropological conceptions, which function as assumptions of different fields of knowledge, would be the adoption and experience of the ground-motive,

---

Works, Series B – Volume 16, Paideia Press, 2012, 124.
28. Ricardo Quadros Gouvêa, *O lado bom do calvinismo*, p. 279.
29. Herman Dooyeweerd, *In the Twilight of Western Thought*, Collected Works, Series B – Volume 16, Paideia Press, 2012, 127.

which is absolutely antithetical: the Christian principle of creation, fall and redemption. For the reformed philosopher, this ground-motive proclaims the unbreakable unity of the human being, starting from his religious centre, directed to an idea of origin.

Given this definition, wouldn't it be plausible to think that Christian theology is the science that can guide human beings in this process? Would it not be a form of neo-scholasticism? The relationship between philosophy, theology, and knowledge of God and of self is going to be discussed in the next section.

3.3 The Relationship Between Philosophy and Theology

Since it is stated that the knowledge of self and reality depend on the knowledge of God, not in a natural way – as in Aquinas – but in line with the *word-revelation* of God himself, the impression one gets is that philosophy will be, necessarily, subordinated to theology. This relationship and the differentiation of terms is an important point in understanding the Dooyeweerdian philosophical proposal.

First, it is necessary to distinguish theology and religion. Although for most theologians the difference is clear, given that theology is always understood as *a second act*, not being religion itself, but the articulated reflection on aspects of religion, there still seems to be a lot of confusion among those unfamiliar with theology, insofar as they do not make such a distinction.

In Dooyeweerd, since religion is defined in terms of the orientation of the *heart* towards an absolute, it is possible to affirm that religion is a presupposition that acts in the construction of theoretical thought, which is not the same as to affirm that theology is an assumption. For him, in the theological enterprise itself – theoretical thinking – there is a religious presupposition. Such an assumption cannot be the object of analysis, not even of theology. What, therefore, would be the object of theology?

For Dooyeweerd, the biblical religious motive, revealed in the scriptures, *creation-fall-redemption*, cannot be the theoretical object of theology. For him, "its acceptance or rejection is a matter of life or death to us, and not a question of theoretical reflection."[30] Therefore, like God and the human ego, biblical revelation is not the object of theology." The reason is that the special sciences cannot reflect on their own perspectives. In another passage, Dooyeweerd reflects on this:

> Can Christian dogmatic theology in its own purview provide us with this philosophical total view? If so, then it cannot be a special science, but must - in line with the Augustinian conception - be considered to be identical to Christian philosophy. But this solution of the age-old problem concerning the relation between theology and philosophy is unacceptable, both from the philosophical and from the theological point of view.[31]

Thus, as a *special science*, the scientific object of theology belongs to a modal aspect present in the time horizon of human experience. Its object is limited to time and cannot be supratemporal. Thus, "[...] this modal experiential aspect that delimits the specific theological point of view can be no other than the aspect of *faith*."[32] In Dooyeweerd, therefore, the Word of God cannot be confused with the object of theology, since "[...] this very confusion has given rise to the falsely equating dogmatic theology with the doctrine of Holy Scripture, and to the false conception of theology as the necessary mediator between God's Word and the believers."[33]

---

30. Herman Dooyeweerd, *In the Twilight of Western Thought*, Collected Works, Series B – Volume 16, Paideia Press, 2012, 86.

31. Ibid., 2012, 89.

32. *Ibid.*, 92.

33. *Ibid.*, 93.

WHAT HAS AMSTERDAM TO DO WITH ATHENS?

According to Ricardo Quadros Gouvêa:

> Theologians are often not interested in philosophy and are sometimes unaware of the philosophical notions that are present in their theological formulations. One of the things that most shocks theologians in reformational thinking is the displacement of theology as the queen of sciences and its repositioning as one science among the others, with philosophy taking its rightful place, by definition, as the *scientia scientiarum,* science of sciences.[34]

Furthermore, for Dooyeweerd, the biblical motive of creation in God, of falling into sin and of redemption through Jesus Christ, is addressed to the human heart, possessing an unbreakable integral character, the dissolution of which cannot be worked out analytically. As an absolute, the religious constitutes an indissoluble antithesis. However, in the Dutch philosopher's conception, the supratemporal word-revelation manifests itself in the order of time. It is precisely these expressions in modal aspects that become the object of special sciences, in the case of theology, the modal aspect of faith (pistic).

Faith, in Dooyeweerd, is part of the structure of creation, constituting one of the modes of our experience. From this, it would be groundless to claim that some people have faith and others do not. What happens, due to sin, is that faith can take an apostate direction. Explaining the place of the pistic aspect in his cosmonomy, Dooyeweerd points out that:

> [...] faith-aspect occupies an entirely exceptional place in the order of creation; it is the limiting aspect that even in the kernel of its modal sense refers beyond the temporal order, towards the religious center of our existence and the divine Origin of all that has been created.[35]

---

34. Ricardo Quadros Gouvêa, *O lado bom do calvinismo*, 272.
35. Herman Dooyeweerd, *In the Twilight of Western Thought,* Collected

With this definition of faith, Dooyeweerd rejects both the position of the Swiss theologian Karl Barth (1886-1968), of faith as an entirely new creative act of God, as well as the scholastic view of faith as a gift from God to the human mind. In the Dooyeweerdian conception, both the scholastic position as the Barthian one are permeated by the dualism of nature and grace, which makes the scholastics synthesize philosophy and theology and the Barthians establish an antithetical relationship between these two subjects. Commenting on Karl Barth's view, Dooyeweerd asserts: "[...] this dualistic view betrays the after-effects of the Occamistic Nominalism, which has especially influenced the Lutheran view concerning the impossibility of a Christian philosophy."[36]

For Dooyeweerd, the articles of faith are the object of theological science. He exemplifies this definition by presenting the following themes: "[...] the significance of the *imago Dei* before and after the fall, the relation between creation and sin and that of particular grace to common grace, that of the union of the two natures in Jesus Christ."[37] Now, this is a very controversial point in the Dooyeweerdian explanation. Carvalho notes that "[...] if the operation of the word-revelation takes place through the mediation of human speech, one must admit that the scientific explanation of the articles of faith is certainly able to clarify its meaning and eliminate distortions of understanding."[38] Thus, it seems that postulating a complete separation between revelation through the Word and theological explanation would not be plausible.

Philosophy and theology, although influenced by the same re-

Works, Series B – Volume 16, Paideia Press, 2012, 95.

36. *Ibid.*, 98.

37. *Ibid.*, 100 and 101.

38. Guilherme de Carvalho, nota de rodapé 21. In: *Ibid.*, 195-6.

ligious presupposition, have different areas of study. For this reason, in Dooyeweerd, to speak of a Christian philosophy is not to speak of a Christian theology, but of a philosophy that is under the guidance of the Christian ground-motive. In this sense, the object of philosophy differs from the object of theology – while the first seeks to understand the structure of reality, in its coherence between the different modes of experience, the second reflects on one of these modal aspects, which is that of faith.

Having explored the main elements that constitute Herman Dooyeweerd's reformational philosophical program, it is now time to investigate another central element of his thought, the concept of *religious ground-motives*, which, according to the Dutch author, constitutes the foundation that explains the unfolding of the historical process and the formation of culture. That is the purpose of the next chapter.

4

WHAT HAS BABEL TO DO WITH JERUSALEM?

The Roots of Western Culture

THE THEME OF THE historical and cultural development of Western civilization permeates Herman Dooyeweerd's reflection. He was concerned with the base upon which cultural ideas and practices took shape in the history of the West, from the emergence of philosophy in Greek civilization until the mid-twentieth century, the period of his philosophical production.

The questions *What moves history?* and *What is its driving force?* are not new ones. For many, the answer can be as direct as: nature, God, free human will, chance, and so on. For Dooyeweerd, underlying the way in which the answer to these questions are given, there is a notion of *arché* or an *idea of origin*.

Before exploring the Doeeweerdian answer in more depth regarding history and cultural development, I would like to present three examples of answers given to these questions, which represent powerful narratives of how to think about cultural development and the historical process, which could be categorized as *reductionisms*. They are: *biologism, economism* and *dataism*.

4.1 Biologism

Firstly, it is important to state that the term *biologism* does not refer to all biological explanations, as if biology were the problem. However, as already mentioned in this work, when a field of knowledge tries to reduce any explanation of meaning to its own field, subordinating other fields, and conceiving them as subproducts, there we have a reductionism.

The biological explanation becomes biologism when it states that the most powerful driving force of history is biological *survival*. An example of an author that falls under this classification is Richard Dawkins and his *Selfish Gene*. Dawkins starts his book thus:

> If higher space creatures ever visit Earth, the first question they will ask in order to assess the level of our civilization will be: "Have they discovered evolution yet?" Living organisms had existed on earth, never knowing why, for more than three billion years before the truth finally dawned on one of them. His name was Charles Darwin. To be fair, others had slight hints of the truth, but it was Darwin who first organized a coherent and convincing description of why we exist.[1]

It is interesting to observe the religious language that the British biologist uses to speak about truth. His description of the theory of evolution and the role of Darwin has almost the character of a reve-

---

1. Richard Dawkins, *O gene egoísta* (São Paulo: Companhia das Letras, 2007).

lation. Similarly, Dawkins' philosophical narrative connects his idea of origin to the meaning of human existence. The author continues:

> Darwin made it possible for us to respond reasonably to the curious child. We no longer need to seek superstition when facing deep problems: Is there a meaning to life? What do we exist for? Who is man? After enunciating the last of these questions, the eminent zoologist G. G. Simpson explained it this way: the point I want to stress is that all attempts to answer this question before 1859 are worthless and it would be better if we ignored them completely.[2]

When he supports the assertion that all knowledge produced before Darwin is worthless, Dawkins tries to turn his thesis into an indissoluble and absolute antithesis. He rejects both philosophy and any form of what he calls religious or superstitious thinking. In his grammar, morality, aesthetics, transcendence, love, etc. are mere subproducts – epiphenomena – of the biological substrate. From a Dooyeweerdian perspective, we could say that there is a reductionism in operation. Commenting on Dawkins' work, the British theologian Graham Ward notes that Dawkins fabricates a *conceptual idol*,[3] a modern and sophisticated form of idolatry, whose result is still what is described in Psalm 115.

4.2 Economicism

The second example of an answer to the question about what drives history comes from the sociology of Karl Marx. For the 19th century political economist, relations in society could be divided into two distinct parts. Marx believed that there is a substrate, a foundational ground – base – upon which other phenomena emerge. For

---

2. Ibid.
3. Graham Ward, Lecture *Against Idolatry*, Available in: https://www.youtube.com/watch?v=7Amp-u2cFWY.

him, what drives history and social change are the economic and labour relations engendered in the production of material work. Other aspects of human life such as culture, religion, the state, ethics, etc. are derived from these material base working relations. He calls whatever emerges from the base "*superstructure*", where things merely reflect what happens at the base.

At the opening of *the Communist Manifesto*, written in partnership with Friedrich Engels in 1848, Marx declares:

> The history of all hitherto existing society is the history of class struggles. Freeman and slave, patrician and plebeian, lord and serf, guildmaster and journeyman, in a word, oppressor and oppressed, stood in constant opposition to one another, carried on an uninterrupted, now hidden, now open fight, that each time ended, either in the revolutionary reconstitution of society at large, or in the common ruin of the contending classes.[4]

For Marx, therefore, the most fundamental element in reality is a power struggle, expressed in the class conflict. It gives history its dynamism and movement. In his day, mid-nineteenth century, Marx claimed that the ruling class, the bourgeoisie – those who owned the means of production – oppressed and exploited the dominated class, the proletariat – supposedly those who did not have the means of material production. Thus, the class struggle would be per excellence the *locus* where history really happens.

It is not within the scope of this work to explore how the thinking of Rousseau and Hegel had an enormous influence on Marx's intellectual production, however, it is important to note that following Hegel, Marx believed that history has a *telos*, that is, it goes in a certain direction. In his understanding, it would inevitably undergo

---

4. Karl Marx and Friedrich Engels, *O manifesto do Partido Comunista* (São Paulo: Paz e Terra, 1998), 9.

a revolution in order to arrive at what he believed to be a *communist state*, a kind of restored Rousseauian *state of nature*.

In this manner, Marxist thinking attempts to explain change within the social order as well as in the whole of reality by claiming that social conflict lies at the very centre of all dynamics in history. It is, therefore, an economic reductionism, once it interprets every other aspect of reality as subordinated to the social conflict connected to labour divisions throughout humanity's history.

4.3 Dataism

The third example, more recent, but which has been spreading rapidly as a theoretical perspective, is articulated in the book *Homo Deus*, written by Yuval Harari, professor of history at the Hebrew University of Jerusalem. The book was a *bestseller* for several weeks in Europe and the USA when released in 2016. His book aims at the general public, in an accessible language, without using overly technical terms. Harari's work could be categorized largely within a broad renewal of hope in technology as a means of progress, and more specifically as a defence of *dataism*.

The book is basically a presentation of what he describes as the *new religion of humanity*, namely, *dataism*. A religion of data, information, and algorithms. Harari defends the idea that the *telos* of history is the constant increase in the flow of information. He believes that quantifying everything will improve human life.

> Dataism [...] like all religion [...] has its practical commandments. First and foremost, a data scientist must maximize the flow of data by connecting more and more to the media, producing and consuming more information.[5]

---

5. Yuval Harari, *Homo Deus: A Brief History of Tomorrow* (Penguin Random House, 2017), 334.

With an ironic and extremely simplistic approach to both philosophy and Christianity, the author promulgates the belief that the era of religion and the era of humanism have come to an end and are giving way to the era of *algorithms*. In another passage in the book, Harari asserts: "[Humanism] ordered: *listen to your feelings, they will tell you what to do*, but dataism says: *listen to the algorithms, they know you better than you know yourself*."[6]

Harari's perspective can be framed as mentioned above as a new utopia rooted in technology as a religious redeemer of mankind, a belief that has gained adherents in the so-called *transhumanist* movement.[7] The reduction at play here is centred around the reduction of reality and history to the flow of information, or data.

4.4 The Driving Force of History in Dooyeweerd

For the Dutch philosopher, in his reformational perspective, the driving force of history is located in what he calls the *religious ground-motives*. He explains that:

> Scripture teachs us not only that the heart or soul is the religious centre of the entire individual and temporal existence of man but also that each man is created in the religious community of mankind. [...] This is a spiritual community; it is governed and maintained by a religious spirit that works in it as a central force.[8]

The *religious ground-motives* can be defined, thus, as collective religious directions that reflect the fundamental beliefs of a civilization and culture. Furthermore, Dooyeweerd believed that *history* represents the *formative aspect* of human development. In it, culture is generated and oriented in a particular direction.

---

6. *Ibid.*, 454.
7. See https://humanityplus.org/
8. Herman Dooyeweerd, *Roots of Western Culture*, 1979, 30.

Based on the Dooyeweerdian conception of reality, to think about culture and its development within the historical aspect includes, necessarily, the analysis of religion, because for him, the religious is the basis on which culture builds and creates its artifacts. In this sense, his view is very close to that of the theologian Paul Tillich, when he affirms that *religion is the substratum of culture*.[9]

Tillich's approximation to the Dutch philosopher's perspective is also clearly seen in the concept of religion. Paul Tillich's definition of religion is comprehensive and universal, since it seeks not to identify religion with any particular aspect, that is, it does not reduce religion to morality, cognition, aesthetics, etc., but understands it as the dimension of depth that permeates and transcends all these aspects, orienting itself to an *unconditioned* – an *ultimate concern*.[10]

By permeating the whole of life, religion, for Tillich, gives form to culture. Thus, the dualisms and separatisms between religion and culture, sacred and profane, for example, are rejected by the German theologian. He reacts against *autonomy* and *heteronomy*, proposing a *theonomy*, that is, the centrality and return of God to the cultural scene. In this sense, Tillich's Christ is the transformer of culture.[11]

This perspective is similar to Dooyeweerdian thought, in that it also comprehends culture as an expression of something previous, which is precisely religion, understood as the orientation of the heart towards an absolute. In addition, the transformation and reformation of culture were and are emphases of the neo-Calvinists, who interpret it from the idea of a creational cultural mandate to produce artifacts that glorify the Creator.

For Dooyeweerd, there are four *religious ground-motives* that

---

9. Rosino Gibellini, *A teologia do século XX*, 85.
10. *Ibid.*, 87.
11. *Ibid.*, 102.

shape both thought and culture in the Western world: the Greek *matter and form,* the Christian *creation, fall and redemption,* the scholastic *nature and grace* and the humanist *nature and freedom.* For him, "[these ground-motives] have been the deepest driving forces behind the entire cultural and spiritual development in the West."[12] Commenting on the foundations of philosophical thinking, he asserts that "[…] the real starting-point of philosophical thought cannot be the ego in itself, which is an empty notion. It can only be the religious basic motive, operative in the ego as the center of our temporal horizon of experience."[13]

In the Dooyeweerdian perspective, of all religious ground-motives, the only one that would be synthetically indissoluble is that of *creation, fall and redemption,* this being the true metanarrative of human history. The other three would be apostate and idolatrous. In his words: "The essence of an idolatrous spirit is that it draws the heart of man from the true God and replaces Him with a creature. By deifying what is created, idolatry absolutizes the relative and considers self-sufficient what is not self-sufficient."[14]

The alternation between the dialectical poles of these ground-motives would configure the dynamics of development and differentiation of thought and culture in the West. In this sense, Dooyeweerd postulates that the Greek religious ground-motive of *matter and form* represents a powerful force for historical development, while, even though it has undergone adaptations and modifications, it has continued to operate - as it has been synthesized - in the scholastic and humanistic ground-motives.

---

12. Herman Dooyeweerd, *Roots of Western Culture,* 1979, 9.
13. Herman Dooyeweerd, *In the Twilight of Western Thought,* Collected Works, Series B – Volume 16, Paideia Press, 2012, 25.
14. Herman Dooyeweerd, *Roots of Western Culture,* 1979, 13.

4.5 Religious Ground-Motives
4.5.1 Matter and Form

In his reflection, the Amsterdam philosopher tries to problematize the ancient Greek context, understanding it as something more complex than some modern simplifications tried portraying. Dooyeweerd says that at the centre of different aspects of Greek culture, including the rise of philosophy, there was a crucial religious issue, related to the origin of all things. At the heart of the dispute over the idea of origin was a dualism between *matter* and *form,* which could not be resolved by theoretical categories since its roots extended to pre-theoretical religious beliefs.

Bearing in mind that the religion in Dooyeweerd is related to the search for the *arché,* that is, the origin of both human beings and reality, the fundamental conflict in ancient Greece would have been the religious confrontation regarding the idea of origin, containing, on the one hand, the ancient religions of nature and, on the other, the new cultural religion of the Olympic gods.

The motive of *matter* was based on "[the] deification of a formless, cyclical stream of life."[15] From that point on, the Greek idea of time itself constituted a conception of cyclical time that was repeated just like the very cycles of nature. This vital flow could not be recognized and studied in a rational way, since it was identified as *Anangké*[16]. Therefore, for Dooyeweerd, the gods were not identified with personalities, but "[...] the nature gods were always fluid and invisible."[17] Another expression of this flow was *Moira,* whose meaning was an inexorable destiny.

---

15. Herman Dooyeweerd, The *Roots of Western Culture,* 1979, 17.
16. From the Greek ἀνάγκη, it means blind fate. It was part of Homer's mythology.
17. Herman Dooyeweerd, *The Roots of Western Culture,* 1979, 16.

Nevertheless, a new religious form originated in Greece: the *religion of culture*, with its cult of form, harmony, and measure. This religious novelty gained strength with the development of the city-states in Greece, in which its centre was on Mount Olympus. According to Dooyeweerd, this new religion of form gained its articulation in Homer's heroic poetry.

> The Olympian gods left 'mother earth' and her cycle of life behind. They were immortal, radiant gods of form: invisible, personal, and idealized cultural forces. Mount Olympus was their home. Eventually the cultural religion found its highest Greek expression in the Delphic god Apollo, the lawgiver [...]. [Homer was concerned] to curb the wild and impassioned worship of Dionysus, the god of wine, with the normative principle of form that characterized Apollo worship.[18]

Dooyeweerd argues that, in the works of Homer and Hesiod, an attempt is made to harmonize these two ideas of origin, in an effort to explain the Olympic gods as evolved forms of the gods of nature. In this sense, the Greek conception would have established a fundamental idea of origin, a principle: "[...] all that comes into being is *chaos* and *formless*."[19]

However, in an attempt to reconcile the religion of nature – *matter* – and the cultural religion – *form* – the *Moira*, previously identified as blind fate, assumes under the banner of the cultural gods a new model: "[...] *Moira* actually became a principle of order."[20] Although, its origin was older than the Olympic gods themselves, going back to a formless and impersonal state. Such was the tension and dualism present in the religious idea of origin in Greek civilization.

---

18. *Ibid.*, 17.
19. *Ibid.*, 18.
20. *Ibid.*, 18.

In the Dooyeweerdian conception, the central contradiction between these two poles, *nature* and *culture,* was in the inability of cultural religion to deal with the issues of death and life, since the gods themselves were subjected to this insurmountable cycle. Thus, even though the official religion of Greece in the sixth century BC was the one of the Olympic gods, the 'cult of mysteries' was very popular, practiced by the Greek population in a private sphere. In this sense, «[...] criticism against it [religion of form] grew more and more outspoken in intellectual circles and the sophists, the Greek ‹enlightened› thinkers of the fifth century."[21]

A very important point arising from this is that the distinction between *form* and *matter* would have influenced the well-known notion of Greek dualism between *body* and *soul,* which would later clash with the Christian conceptions of body and soul, permeating also the idea of a separation between the natural world (material) and the supernatural (ideal).

Thus, Dooyeweerd thinks that Plato's philosophy, for example, was grounded in the basic belief of an origin of all things rooted in this dialectical tension between *matter* and *form.* The platonic *demiurge* is not a deity that creates all things, but it is the divinity that gives *shape* to all, once it receives from *Anangké* a matter that has no form or meaning.

Plato's idea of the divine, therefore, is that of a *divine reason,* which organizes and orders the evil flow of deformed life. Similarly, for "[...] Plato's great pupil Aristotle pure form was the divine mind (*nous*), but *Anangké* which permeated matter was still the peculiar cause of everything anomalous and monstrous in the world."[22]

Thus, according to Dooyeweerd, the Greeks recognized a cos-

---

21. *Ibid.,* 19.
22. *Ibid.,* 29.

mic order, without, however, recognizing a divine creation. What they did was to absolutize a relative aspect present in creation. For them, the rational principle was the organizing centre for a meaningless matter. Therefore, from this central ground-motive their philosophical and cultural roots were derived, based on a mistaken direction of the idea of origin.

4.5.2 Creation, Fall and Redemption

Unlike the Greek motif of matter and form, Christianity's ground-motive is, as stated by Dooyeweerd, the only one that does not recognize a tension - a *dualism* - between form and matter. It is revealed through Christ's redemptive action and gives true *insight* into whom God is and the true origin of everything. From a Christian viewpoint, all the cosmos is God's creation. Creation, the material world, is not corrupt in itself, as it brings with it the sense and significance attributed by the Creator. "This creation is ordered by the Creator's will and reflects His glory, so that, in its structure, there is an order of laws, or a *cosmonomy*."[23]

The reality of evil or that which causes fissures and suffering in the created order is a direct result of the *fall*, which can be interpreted as an apostate direction of the natural human religious impulse. The disobedience of human beings has caused an alienation from the Creator, from ourselves and from all creation. Sin, in Dooyeweerd's view, has not affected the structure of creation, but, rather, the human relationship with it.[24]

---

23. Guilherme Carvalho, "Sociedade, justiça e política na filosofia de cosmovisão cristã." In: Maurício Cunha et al. (Org.), *Cosmovisão cristã e transformação*, 128.
24. See Herman Dooyeweerd, *No crepúsculo do pensamento ocidental*, p. 86; Guilherme Carvalho, "Sociedade, justiça e política na filosofia de cosmovisão cristã." In: Maurício Cunha et al. (Org.), *Cosmovisão cristã e transformação*, 128.

The third element present in the Christian ground-motive is that of the redemption of all things in Christ. Redemption is understood as the redirection of the human religious centre towards the true God, in a process of re-creating and restoring the relationships that were distorted by sin. Commenting on this, Carvalho states that "[...] redemption *does not mean the addition of a special grace*, but simply the reconstitution of God's original purpose."[25]

The apostle Paul, in the letter to the Colossians, writes:

> The Son is the image of the invisible God, the firstborn over all creation. For in him all things were created: things in heaven and on earth, visible and invisible, whether thrones or powers or rulers or authorities; all things have been created through him and for him. He is before all things, and in him all things hold together. And he is the head of the body, the church; he is the beginning and the firstborn from among the dead, so that in everything he might have the supremacy. For God was pleased to have all his fullness dwell in him, and through him to reconcile to himself all things, whether things on earth or things in heaven, by making peace through his blood, shed on the cross.[26]

Thus, in the affirmation that Christ is the Lord of all created things, the Christian faith differs radically from the Greek view of divinity. The Greek deity gives shape to all things, but it is not related to the origin of matter. In Christ, however, all things hold together. His Lordship extends to all spheres of created reality. Therefore, in highlighting the idea of a God who creates everything that exists, the Christian ground-motive constitutes an *absolute antithesis* in relation to the Greek ground-motive of matter and form, and should not,

---

25. Guilherme Carvalho, "Sociedade, justiça e política na filosofia de cosmovisão cristã." In: Maurício Cunha et al. (Org.), *Cosmovisão cristã e transformação*, 128.

26. Colossians 1:15-20 (NIV)

according to Dooyeweerd, be synthesized with it.[27]

Another important element of this ground-motive is the postulate of the unbreakable unity between the revelation of who God is and of who the human person is. This human identity rooted in the image and likeness of the Creator demonstrates the essentially religious character of human life. The Dutch philosopher also notes that the motif of *creation, fall and redemption* "[...] does not depend on human theology. Its radical sense can only be explained by the Holy Spirit, operating in the heart [...] within the communion of the invisible Catholic church."[28]

4.5.3 Nature and Grace

The third religious driving force of great influence in the West was the result, according to Dooyeweerd, of a great synthesis of the Greek ground-motive of matter and form with the one believed by Christianity. In church history, one can identify the *Gnostic* movement as the first one that tried to introduce Greek dualism into the Christian worldview in an attempt to separate the Creator God, who would be in a lower sphere, identified with the God of the Old Testament, from the 'higher God', which presents itself as the redeeming God, as expressed in the New Testament.[29]

In this sense,

> Many Gnostics denied the incarnation of Jesus, for they said that God could not have become matter without being contaminated. Therefore, Jesus only appeared to be human, however, his body was not real, only apparent. The Gospel of John, like the Johannine epistles, clearly fight

---

27. Herman Dooyeweerd, *Roots of Western Culture*, 1979, 29.
28. Herman Dooyeweerd, *2012*. P.31.
29. Herman Dooyeweerd, *Roots of Western Culture*, 1979, 112.

the mistake of this Gnostic teaching.[30]

The Dutch philosopher articulated this influence when he writes about the Greek Fathers of the primitive Church:

> The Greek church fathers conceived of creation as a result of the divine activity of giving form to matter. They could not consider matter divine. Consequently, they hesitated to recognize the Word, through which all things were created and which became flesh in Jesus Christ [...] Accordingly, they degraded the Word (the *Logos*) to a 'semigod' who,' as 'mediator' of creation, stood between God and creature [...]. [They] also placed contemplative theoretical knowledge of God above faith."[31]

Dooyeweerd argues that this idea gained its well-known form with the medieval philosopher Thomas Aquinas (1225-1274) and his synthesis between Aristotelian philosophy and the Christian faith. Dooyeweerd also pays attention to a previous philosopher, whose work is in the early medieval period: Augustine of Hippo (354-430).

As a reformed thinker, the Dutch philosopher has in Augustine a great source of inspiration. The main point of convergence with the Bishop of Hippo concerns his rejection of the idea of the autonomy of philosophy in relation to the Christian faith. Augustine also maintained the biblical ground-motive of *creation, fall and redemption*, advocating a good creation that is marred by sin, but redeemed in Christ.

However, he would have proposed a mistaken solution to the problem of the relationship between philosophy and Chris-

---

30. Fernando Albano, *Dualismo corpo/alma na teologia pentecostal*. (Dissertação de Mestrado. São Leopoldo: EST, 2010), 2. Veja também: Jo 1.1-18; 1 Jo 4.1-3.

31. Herman Dooyeweerd, *Roots of Western Culture*, 1979, 113.

tian faith. By mistakenly identifying dogmatic theology with the Christian faith, Augustine believed that Christian theology was the ground-motive of philosophy. "Thus, theology functioned as *regina scientiarum*, or 'the queen of sciences'."[32] From a cosmonomic perspective, theology as a special science cannot take the place of philosophy or even be confused with the biblical ground-motive.

In the second stage, with *scholasticism*, especially in the works of Thomas Aquinas, there is a distinction between philosophy and theology, but for other reasons. From a Thomistic perspective, there is a clear separation between nature and supernature, that is, between a natural world and the supernatural world. By inheriting an Aristotelian conception of nature, "The scholastics argued that whatever was subject to birth and death, including man, was composed of matter and form."[33]

The *scholastics* maintained that in creation the Creator would have given the human being a supernatural gift – a grace, a superhuman faculty of will and thought (rationality), with which the human being would relate to God Himself. Nevertheless, "[...] humanity lost this gift with the fall, and consequently was reduced to a simple 'human nature', with weaknesses inherent in it."[34] The central point of this interpretation is that human nature, although fallen in sin, would continue to be defined as a *rational soul* capable of comprehending the things with the sphere of nature. Hence the idea of a *natural* reason. In this way, "[...] the sphere of nature is seen as an autonomous reality."[35]

---

32. Guilherme Carvalho, "Sociedade, justiça e política na filosofia de cosmovisão cristã." In: Maurício Cunha et al. (Org.), *Cosmovisão cristã e transformação*, 133.

33. Herman Dooyeweerd, *Roots of Western Culture*, 1979, 116.

34. *Ibid.*

35. Guilherme Carvalho, "Sociedade, justiça e política na filosofia de cosmovisão cristã." In: Maurício Cunha et al. (Org.), *Cosmovisão cristã e*

Based on this worldview, the scholastics believed that natural reason, despite the fall, continued with its original capacities, being unable only to reflect on divine realities, which should be received in the revelation, through faith. [...] Faith should guide reason so that it understands the truths of the gospel, *but such guidance was not considered necessary for reason to understand nature.*[36]

The introduction of this dualism in Christian thought resulted in the idea of a supposedly independent and autonomous sphere in creation, which would give space for the next step in the advancement of Western thought: the pole of nature devouring the pole of grace.[37] This is the basis, in the Dooyeweerdian interpretation, of the idea of a secular world. The medieval *great synthesis* had its influence in the West until the 16th century, marked by the *nominalist* movement and the emergence of a new ground-motive, that of *nature* and *freedom*.

4.5.4 Nature and Freedom

If the scholastic ground-motive that prevailed in Europe for several centuries was the one that maintained a dialectical relationship between nature and grace, the one prevalent in the modern period had its origin at the same time, with the work of the British Franciscan William of Ockham (1280-1347). Ockham criticised the idea of a synthesis between Greek philosophy and faith. Starting from the idea of a Creator that is sovereign – *absoluta potestas* –, he tried to attack the Thomist belief that resembled the Greek deification of reason.[38]

As a result of this assumption, Ockham separated thoroughly

---

   transformação, 134.

36. *Ibid.*
37. Francis Schaeffer, *A morte da razão* (Viçosa, MG: Ultimato, 2014), 17.
38. Herman Dooyeweerd, *Roots of Western Culture*, 1979, 138.

these two dimensions: nature and grace, asserting the arbitrariness of divine law expressed in the decalogue. Such a postulate contradicted the Aristotelian-Thomist idea of a natural reason capable of attaining the knowledge of God.

The Occamist idea had a great impact on the relationship of the medieval Roman Catholic ecclesiastical structure with society, the State and also with the philosophical endeavour. We can say that with William of Ockham there was a change in the centre of gravity of the idea of power and sovereignty. Thus,

> The future presented only two options: one could either return to the scriptural ground motive of the Christian religion or, in line with the new motive of nature severed from the faith of the church, establish a modern view of life concentrated on the religion of human personality. The first path led to the Reformation; the second path led to modern humanism. In both movements after-effects of the Roman Catholic motive of nature and grace continued to be felt for a long time [39]

In the Protestant Reformation the effects of Occamism and its ground-motive of *nature and grace* – although in a new form, in the motive of *freedom* – were felt in the Lutheran idea of the opposition between law and gospel. Herman Dooyeweerd asserts that "[...] in Luther's thought [the law was deprecated] as the order for 'sinful nature' and thus began to view 'law' in terms of a religious *antithesis* to 'evangelical grace'."[40] What Dooyeweerd calls a *Protestant scholasticism* would later influence the *dialectical theology* of Karl Barth, very popular in the days of Dooyeweerd.

As already mentioned, such a separation between *nature* and *grace* would result in the development of modern humanism, whose main element is the postulate that nature has a reality inde-

---

39. *Ibid.*, 139.
40. *Ibid.*, 140.

pendent of the sphere of grace. Therefore, faith – whose functioning would be exclusive to that independent sphere of nature – would be a private matter of the human being.

This supposed autonomy of thought would have its religious meaning camouflaged. Here is the main point of the Dooyeweerdian critique: "Since Kant ... the dogma of the autonomy [...] of thought [...] has been presented as a purely philosophical theme concerning the relationship between theoretical reason and practice, a topic also discussed in Greek and scholastic philosophies."[41]

In this context, the *Renaissance* was, for Dooyeweerd, the movement that articulated the idea of a conception of a new human being: "[...] this personality was thought of as absolute in itself and considered the only ruler of its own destiny and the destiny of the world."[42] This ideal of human freedom and autonomy came into conflict with the new modern conception of the nature, no longer the continuous and formless flow of the Greeks, but a deterministic nature, full of causal laws, which could be rationally studied through the eyes of reason.

> The mechanistic world-image constructed under the primacy of the nature-motive, aiming at the sovereign domination of the world, left no room for autonomous freedom of human personality in its practical activity. Nature and freedom appeared to be opposite motives in the humanistic starting-point.[43]

The Doyeweerdian position is that these two dialectical poles of humanism cannot find an ultimate synthesis, since they are aspects of reality made into absolutes. The Kantian answer to the problem

---

41. Herman Dooyeweerd, *No crepúsculo do pensamento ocidental*, 88.
42. *Ibid.*, 89.
43. Herman Dooyeweerd, In the Twilight of Western Thought, 2012, 35.

of determinism of nature, for example, had been a separation between *nature* and *freedom*, insofar as "[...] man's autonomous freedom does not belong to the sensory field of nature, but to the suprasensory field of ethics, which is not governed by natural laws, but by norms."[44] With Kant, the pole of *freedom* was granted precedence.

Kantian dualism would have been overcome by *post-Kantian idealism*, which sought an ultimate synthesis between these two poles. It was with Friedrich Hegel (1770-1831) that the attempt of a synthesis *via* history was undertaken.

Hegel's philosophy is a universalist philosophy at its root. Its objective was to develop large explanatory frameworks that covered several areas. Likewise, Hegel had a teleological concept of history, which coerced him into writing and thinking big schemes that fit different contexts within the same framework of evolutionary progress, towards an ultimate *telos*, in which the whole of humanity was inserted. For him, one must look for a universal *telos* in history, the goal of the world, a reason.[45] The main idea developed in the work *The Reason in Universal History* is that humanity is moving towards the full consciousness of freedom, its maximum development, achieved by the development of reason, which is not a particular reason, but the one that concerns a totality. Hegel tries to demonstrate, mainly through historical analysis, how this *universal reason* that governs history has manifested itself in the context of different peoples.

The language used by Hegel in this work is often religious, with analogies and examples taken mainly from Christianity and the Bible. There seems to be an equivalence between Hegel's concept of universal reason and the Christian idea of providence.

---

44. Herman Dooyeweerd, 2010, 93.
45. See Georg Wilhelm Friedrich Hegel, *A razão na história universal: Introdução à filosofia da história universal* (Lisboa: Edições 70, 1995).

> In universal history, however, we deal with individuals who are peoples, with wholes that are states; therefore, we cannot, so to speak, remain in the triviality of faith in providence, nor in the merely abstract, indeterminate faith, which persists only in the universal statement that there is a providence that governs the world, but without wanting to pass on to the determined.[46]

In a way, Hegel secularizes the idea of divine providence at work in the world, which would govern the course of human history, replacing it with a concept that, according to him, would not be too abstract, like the Christian one. Meanwhile, in the post-Hegelian philosophical context, a historicist view of the temporal world was developed, according to Dooyeweerd, which "[...] reduced all other aspects of our experience to the historical aspect."[47] This perspective would highlight the pole of freedom of the ground-motive of nature and freedom.

Dooyeweerd points out that the constant change from one pole to the other within this ground-motive had a big shift "[...] in the middle of the 19th century, the German freedom-idealism broke down, and gave place to a naturalistic positivism. The nature-motive regained the upperhand and the historical mode of thought was transformed into a more complicated kind of natural scientific thinking."[48]

The central point, from a perspective of reformational philosophy is that "[...] contemporary logical positivism and its polar opposite, humanist existentialism, testify to a fundamental crisis in humanistic philosophy."[49] Thus, this constant dialectic plagues the possibilities for a deeper understanding of reality.

---

46. *Ibid.*, 40.
47. Herman Dooyeweerd, *No crepúsculo do pensamento ocidental*, 93.
48. Herman Dooyeweerd, 2012, 36.
49. *Ibid.*, 36.

5

WHAT HAS AMSTERDAM TO DO WITH BRAZIL?

Reflections on Christianity and Culture

THE DUTCH REFORMED TRADITION affirms a direct relationship between religion and culture and the impossibility of them being completely separate. Although there are different perspectives about this relationship, including radical opposition models, one could say that the former is always the foundation of the latter. It is important to reaffirm that, in the Dooyeweerdian categories, religion is the orientation of the *heart* towards an absolute, in which its purpose is to give meaning to human life and experience.

Thus, one realizes that one of the main emphases of the Reformational tradition is that of Christianity as a world-and-life view, with the proclamation of God's sovereignty over the whole of life. In this way, the cultural sphere would be a legitimate sphere of activity and engagement for the Christian in the world, insofar as God's glory should be expressed in it.

5.1 The Case of Brazil

The religious scenario in Brazil has changed considerably in the last 30 years. From being a predominantly Catholic country through different historical periods since the Portuguese colonization, it now bears witness of the growth of evangelicals (*evangélicos*), among which Pentecostals and neo-Pentecostals are worth taking note of because of their exponential growth. In the last census in 2010, 22% of the total population were self-declared *evangélicos* – around 40 million people. Some estimations say that figure reached 30% in 2020. Along with this new scenario, new challenges and theological questions arise. This reflection attempts to address one of the central questions within the Brazilian context: How do *evangélicos* approach culture? Thus, its aim is to discuss the main views of culture among evangelicals in Brazil as well as presenting a Reformational perspective on culture and its growing influence in the Brazilian context.

In his classic work *Christ and Culture*, Richard Niebuhr[1] presents five models of possible relationships between Christianity and culture.[2] This typology is not perfect. Every form of relationship is

---

1. It is important to clarify that this chapter does not aim to interpret the works of Niebuhr. The mention of this classic work is only a general reference of the forms of relationship between Christianity and culture. In the same way, it is important to stress that the typology used by the American theologian presents five models of relationship. The ones not quoted here are *Christ above the culture* and *Christ and culture in paradox*.
2. The lecture Christ and Culture Revisited given by Jock McGregor is

WHAT HAS AMSTERDAM TO DO WITH BRAZIL?

never isolated and disassociated from another, nor from a particular given context with its singularities. This framework could, nonetheless, shed some light on the case of Brazil. Niebuhr's typology of analysis will be used as the interpretative apparatus – just as a general reference – of the Brazilian context. This chapter presents and discusses three different models of approaching culture in Brazil: 1) Christians against culture; 2) Christians of the culture; 3) Christians as culture's reformers. The third one would be a response and alternative to the first two.

With the significant change in its religious matrix – besides being the most Catholic country in the world, Brazil is also the most Pentecostal one – the emergent *evangélicos* have a whole new set of challenges to face. Alongside financial prosperity and the increasing size of the middle class, the classic Latin American theological theme of the poor – especially raised by *Liberation Theology*[3] – seems to give space to new questions as well. One of them is related to the comprehension of culture and how *evangélicos* should approach it.

One of the great dilemmas of Brazilian Christians[4] has to do with their relationship with the world and with its cultural system. Does a Christian belong to this world? It is read in one of the apostle John's letters: "Do not love the world or anything in the world. If anyone loves the world, the love of the Father is not in him."[5] Nevertheless, the same apostle writes in his gospel that: "For God so loved

---

very helpful to understand Niebuhr's ideas and provided some insights for this analysis. Available in <http://labri-ideas library.org/do-download.asp?Lecture=1544>

3. See Gustavo Gutiérrez, *A Theology of Liberation: History, Politics, and Salvation*. Revised Edition with a New Introduction (Maryknoll: Orbis, 1988).

4. The terms Christians and evangelicals (*evangélicos*) are going to be used interchangeably.

5. 1 John 1:15 (NIV)

the world that He gave His one and only son [...]."⁶ Do they mean the same thing? What is the "world" from a Christian standpoint? There seems to be, in the Brazilian context, an enormous confusion between the world as a sinful system and the world as God's creation.

5.2 Christians Against Culture

In this perspective, Christianity and culture are at odds, having no common ground whatsoever. Thus, integration would not be possible. In general, religious groups prone toward charismatic and evangelical expressions of faith are more inclined to this understanding. Much of the emphasis in their preaching is given to personal sanctification defined as separation from the world.⁷

The foundation for such an interpretation about the relationship between Christians and the world – here encompassing the cultural sphere – has its roots in the (Neo-)Platonic dualism of *body* and *soul*.⁸ This dualism, rooted in the Greek *ground-motive* of *matter* and *form*, will have been transformed in the Middle Ages into a new *ground-motive*, the one of *nature* and *grace*. At its core is the fundamental belief that matter – the visible world – is evil; in it would be contained the sinful passions that destroy and fight against the soul. The only alternative would be the systematized denying of the body, valuing in its place the attributions of the activities of the soul.

Consequently, what is natural – visible – is understood as a mere distortion of a superior, supernatural reality. This belief is built from

---

6. John 3:16ª (NIV)
7. See the critical perspective of Rick Nañez regarding this position, as well as his study on the origin of this sort of dualism within Christianity. In: Rick Nañez, *Pentecostal de coração e mente: um chamado ao dom divino do intelecto* (São Paulo: Ed. Vida, 2007), 160.
8. See Fernando Albano, *Dualismo corpo/alma na teologia pentecostal. Dissertation*. Programa de Pós-Graduação em Teologia EST: São Leopoldo, 2010, 13.

and upon Plato's *theory of forms*. In his classical work *The Republic*,[9] Plato presents his famous allegory of the cave as an illustration of his philosophical outlook. In his Socratic dialogues, Plato understands the world we can see and experience as a prison, and the exercise of reason as a window opening to a superior and elevated reality, a way out of the bodily imprisonment. Such a view seems to find parallels to the identification – present in Brazilian evangelicalism – of the world and its structures as evil things in themselves.[10] Therefore, the abandonment of this world, through spiritual disciplines – understood as invisible ones – would be the model of life and spirituality for Christians.

There seems to be a suspicion or demonization of all cultural production, many thinking it a sinful form of expression. According to Nañez, there is a *mind collapse*,[11] the consequence of which is a form of *fideism* – a reduction of the interpretation of reality to faith categories, in opposition to the acknowledgement of the faith aspect as a part of a broader structure of meaning. In addition, a closer look at the first evangelical missions to Brazil reveals a strong tendency of a separatist accent between Christians and culture.[12] These 19th and

---

9. Platão. *A República*, 514a-517c. In: Danilo Marcondes, *Textos Básicos de Filosofia: dos Pré-socráticos a Wittgenstein*. 2ª ed. (Rio de Janeiro: Jorge Zahar Editor, 2000).
10. It is important to clarify that the reception and adaptation of the Platonic thought is not immediate and direct. It has suffered a significant historical process of transformation, being synthesised with other forms of thinking. In this paper, the establishment of a parallel between Platonic dualism and the evangelical worldview is identified more as a reference to its origins and less as a direct derivation.
11. Rick Nañez, *Pentecostal de coração e mente: um chamado ao dom divino do intelecto* (São Paulo: Ed. Vida, 2007), 187.
12. Certainly, the character of the evangelical missions to Brazil cannot be reduced to this separatism. It is acknowledged here the complexities of the religious and sociological aspects implied in these past events. This

20th-century missions had their origins, mainly, in the United States revival movements.[13]

In North America, those same movements that defended an anti-intellectual attitude came to be known later on as *fundamentalists* once their *fideism* was explicitly clear. In 1925, for example, there occurred the paradigmatic legal case known as the Monkey Trial, in which the state of Tennessee forbade the teaching of the Darwinist theory of evolution for supposedly contradicting the biblical teaching of creation. Under the influence of the debate in the USA, many of the facets of the discussion between Christianity and science in Brazil were rooted in the dualism of creation*ism* and evolution*ism*, inculcating the position that Christians could not assume any other posture than that promulgated by the theory of *intelligent design*.

In the same manner, against the defensive Christian evangelical tendency that fears both the cultural sphere and intellectual activities, there is a tremendous influence of the *positivist*[14] movement in Brazilian academia. As a result, an extremely hostile environment towards any manifestation that would involve religious categories, both in the academic level as well as in the public sphere in general, was generated. From a Dooyeweerdian understanding, the myth of the *religious neutrality of reason* is still at work.

According to the Swiss-Brazilian theologian Rudolf von Sinner, "[…] public universities in Brazil have a tradition of strong reservations against religion and theology."[15] A potential historical ex-

---

analysis is not part of the scope of this book.

13. José Miguez Bonino, *Rostos do Protestantismo Latino-Americano* (São Leopoldo: Ed. Sinodal, 2002), 29.
14. Movement that began in France in the 19th century, whose main author was Auguste de Comte, one of the fathers of Sociology.
15. Rudolf von Sinner, *Teologia Pública no Brasil*. In: Afonso Maria Ligorio Soares; João Décio Passos (Orgs.). *Teologia Pública: Reflexões sobre uma área de conhecimento e sua cidadania acadêmica* (São Paulo: Paulinas,

planation for this posture, in his perspective, is the advent of "[...] eclecticism, brought to Brazil from France (Maine de Biran, Victor Cousin) via Portugal, and of Comte's positivism, which became very influential during the Brazilian empire period [...]"[16].

Another sphere worth paying attention to is the media. Apart from the numerous evangelical TV programmes, channels with exclusively Christian content are multiplying across the country. An evangelical cable network was launched, with the name of *Nossa TV* ("Our TV"). It is associated with a well-known televangelist, Missionary R. R. Soares, in which its chief goal is to be an alternative entertainment for the Brazilian evangelical audience.

Likewise, gospel music is one of the most profitable markets in Brazil.[17] However, there seems to be a constant tension with regards to the artistic sphere. According to Magali do Nascimento Cunha: "One of the marks of gospel music expression called *praise and worship* is the fact that the singers insist that they are not artists, but worshippers."[18] Equally, Cunha points out that for this conception, "The artistic carrier [...] is incompatible with God's purpose [...]"[19].

In spite of its ambiguities, there is a real presence of evangelical cultural production. Nonetheless, the logic of this production follows patterns of a marketing segmentation, not being spread out for the whole culture. An example of this segmentation and differ-

---

2011), 265-276.

16. *Ibid.*, 269.
17. One of the most well-known magazines in Brazil dedicated a full report to this subject <http://veja.abril.com.br/noticia/celebridades/musica-gospel-trinados-fe-e-dinheiro>
18. See Magali do Nascimento Cunha, *A explosão gospel: um olhar das ciências humanas sobre o cenário evangélico no Brasil* (Rio de Janeiro: Mauad X: Instituto Mysterium, 2007), 107.
19. *Ibid.*, 108.

entiation is *Espirítoval*,[20] an evangelical celebration, that in order to oppose the "feast of the flesh" (*Carnival*), would celebrate the "feast of the Spirit." In this distinction, there is a strong exclusivism, given the fact that for the evangelicals the cultural artefacts produced by specific groups are taken as holy, in opposition to the worldly culture that would carry only the fruits of sin.

> The so-called language [of the] world, in the evangelical tradition, [is used to] refer to the space, which is not of the church, of the saved ones, of those who are guarded from evil and sin [...]. The dualism church-world, constituted as a base for the theology and for the action of the Brazilian evangelicals, is conserved even in the midst of the transformations inserted by the composition of pop melodies, sung by pop singers.[21]

This point is in conflict with the idea of *common Grace*, stressed by Abraham Kuyper:

> Whereas the special grace is that one through which God saves the sinner through Jesus Christ, common grace would be that one through which God restricts corruption in the world caused by sin, allowing the development of life and human culture.[22]

The Dutch reformer defended that the common grace given by God allowed every human being – whether Christian or not – to have the capacity of creating good things: cultural artefacts, for instance, that would reflect God's glory. Therefore, cultural productions should not be rejected according to the religious confession

---

20. Available in: <http://www.lagoinha.com/ibl-noticia/adoracao-e-alegria-compoe-o-espiritoval 2014/>
21. Cunha, 2007, 131.
22. Rodomar Ramlow, *O Neocalvinismo Holandês e o Movimento de Cosmovisão Cristã. Dissertação em Teologia*, EST/PPG (São Leopoldo, 2012), 25.

of their authors once they are viewed as an expression of the common grace shed over creation.

5.3 Christians of the Culture

A more attentive look at Brazil's evangelical boom in recent years reveals the growth of neo-Pentecostal churches, as in the case of *Igreja Universal* (*Universal Church of the Kingdom of God*) and *Igreja Internacional da Graça* (*International Church of the Grace of God*). Other evangelical groups include charismatic, youth-oriented churches such as *Bola de Neve Gospel Church* (the SnowBall Gospel Church), which began with a membership of surfers and has now spread to young urban middle-class groups. One of the features of these new ecclesiastical models is to make Christianity attractive for those unfamiliar with church environments. In this, Christianity and the church would need to adapt to the changes, accepting the new form of thinking and the new contemporary cultural artefacts.

Historically, according to Richard Niebuhr, some movements could be identified with the perspective of harmonization between Christ – or Christianity – and culture. It may be that the most well-known has been *liberalism*, even if the author prefers the term *cultural Protestantism*.[23] For the American theologian, "[...] although their fundamental interest has to do with what relates to this word, they do not reject that which transcends this level (other-worldliness), but seek to understand the transcendent kingdom as a continuum in time."[24]

It has to be made clear, however, that there is a significant vacuum between liberalism and the Brazilian neo-Pentecostal movements – the hypothetical similitudes have yet to be discussed – though they

---

23. Richard H. Niebuhr, *Cristo e cultura, Paz e Terra* (Rio de Janeiro, 1967), 111.

24. *Ibid*, 110.

are alike in terms of their approach to certain kinds of cultural dynamics, whether by accepting a particular epistemology based on the neutrality of reason or through the acritical reception of the consumption of society's logic.

Most of the critics of this model have their starting point in the assumption that a simple accommodation between Christianity and culture would affect Christian faith and its fundamental beliefs, orthodoxy, through the distortion of central biblical ideas. In order to understand what sort of distortions it would cause; it would be necessary to understand coherently the main features of our Western culture.

It has been commonplace already to name our times, especially the period beginning after the Second World War, as postmodern. Among the main features of this new configuration would be the loss of meaning of life and reality, both in religious terms and in terms of rationality, resulting in a fragmentation of the idea of truth, which generates disintegration in many levels, especially regarding personal identity, references to which would be lost amid the crisis of metanarratives. As a result, there is a weakening of more universal interpretative categories, opening space for individualistic and relativistic narratives. Such a scenario is responsible for an extreme dynamism, in which its outcome is a constant change.

Having the postmodern paradigm as a reference, many social theorists, philosophers and theologians analyze the Brazilian religious phenomenon by establishing parallels with the individualistic and market-oriented approach of our times, given that "[…] religions and theologies that arise from a postmodern worldview diverge greatly from a biblical orthodoxy […] and from modernity as well."[25]

It is not in the scope of this paper to dive deeper into this ele-

---

25. Robson Ramos, *Evangelização no mercado Pós-Moderno* (Viçosa: Ultimato, 2003), 91.

ment. Nevertheless, the aim here is to indicate a few examples of this *modus operandi* within some Brazilian evangelical movements. The most noticeable example is the prosperity gospel, which could be broadly defined as

> [an] inter-confessional charismatic movement that emphasises physical health and financial prosperity as basic evidence of the divine blessings in the Christian life... [It] is, with no doubt, the highest expression of the accommodation of the Christian life to the capitalist ideal of physical and material prosperity.[26]

One of the pillars of the Christian faith, God's sovereignty as stressed in the reformed context, seems to be shaken by a profound concentration on the individual, who sees God as a means of his personal self-fulfilment. There is an inversion – the individual's will becomes sovereign, supposedly achieved through such religious rituals as the so-called campaigns of spiritual and financial victory, mediated by contemporary techniques of motivation and self-help.

The *modus vivendi* of the church, from this perspective of interaction with culture, transforms the service and its liturgy into a more palatable and acceptable expression for the world, with a very pragmatic agenda of attracting those who are on the outside. In a flyer from an evangelical church in Rio de Janeiro, it is written, as an invitation to its services: "You can come and bring that friend of yours who enjoys electronic music, forró[27] and other rhythms, who loves a good football match and excitement. Let's show them that we know how to party and together worship God!"[28] This is an example

---

26. Alberto R. Timm, In: Fernando Bortolleto Filho, *Teologia da Prosperidade. Dicionário Brasileiro de Teologia* (São Paulo: ASTE, 2008), 966-968.

27. A Brazilian musical rhythm.

28. Available in: http://www.boladeneve.com/eventos/balada-da-zona-sul

of the so-called *gospel nightclub* (*balada* gospel).

From a reformational standpoint, both the total rejection of the cultural dimension or an acritical accommodation of it are not perspectives that reflect the Christian ground motive of *creation, fall* and *redemption*. An alternative is presented in the next section: a panoramic perspective of the reformational proposal of the interaction between Christianity and culture.

5.4 Christians as Culture's Reformers

From a *Reformational* perspective, the Christian religion is constituted by a broad worldview of reality emphasizing the sovereignty of Christ over all of life,[29] based on the affirmation of a complete harmony between God the Creator and God the Redeemer. Subjacent to the cosmonomic philosophy of Herman Dooyeweerd is the theological principle of the *cultural mandate*, which occurred before the *fall*. In this sense, the theology of creation plays an important role in the understanding of the scope of redemption.

Hence, "[...] the comprehension of the cultural mandate is in the account of creation in Genesis. Human beings are created in the image and likeness of God, receiving the order to develop culture."[30] The mandate to *work and care for the garden*[31] would imply a series of complex activities, such as the administration of different techniques of dealing with the land and the development of the necessary tools to work and cultivate it. Social norms would also need to be created in order to organize the process of work.[32]

---

29. See Colossians 1:15-20 (NIV)
30. Ramlow, 2012b, 28.
31. See Genesis 2:15 (NIV)
32. Guilherme de Carvalho, *A objeção reformada ao dogma da autonomia religiosa da razão*. Revista Diálogo e Antítese, Vol. 1, n° 1, 2009, p. 4-53.

The understanding of the cultural mandate is attached to the concept of *vocation*, as stressed by the reformers Martin Luther and John Calvin. Vocation was not confined to the ecclesiastical ministry, but rather every form of work could be a way of glorifying God. As a consequence, a blacksmith gives glory to God while working in the same way that a pastor pleases the Lord when he delivers a sermon during the service. Abraham Kuyper insisted upon a Christianity that would not divide reality between what was considered sacred and profane.[33]

From a reformational Christian understanding of cultural activity, Guilherme de Carvalho observes:

> In contrast with an isolationist form and a synthetic form of evangelicalism, it is necessary to pursue a dialogic-antithetic form of evangelicalism: with a permanent and critical contact with culture, acknowledging its creational and intrinsically good character, but also being aware of the perverse and universal consequences of the fall.[34]

Given that creation is good, its different dimensions express God's will for the creature. Nevertheless, along with this affirmation, the reformed tradition gives importance to the view of the *fall* as *total depravity*,[35] a total distortion of the created order. As stated by Dooyeweerd, the human heart is inclined to a religious ground-motive, seeking for its origin – *arché* – as a way of giving meaning to reality. Whenever the human heart is not oriented to God it expresses its fallen and apostate condition. Such orientation of the heart cre-

---

33. Abraham Kuyper, *Calvinismo* (São Paulo: Cultura Cristã, 2003).
34. Guilherme Carvalho, *O dualismo natureza/graça e a influência do humanismo secular no pensamento social cristão*. In: Maurício Cunha, et al. (Orgs.). *Cosmovisão cristã e transformação: espiritualidade, razão e ordem social* (Viçosa, MG: Ultimato, 2006), pp. 123-174, p. 143.
35. This terminology was created and developed by the Synod of Dort (1618-1619).

ates the only dualism existent in reality: the religious antithesis of the heart, introduced by sin in the fall. The antithetical, therefore, would be at work within the human heart – the religious centre – and not in the external structures of society. This erroneous orientation affects every aspect of life, from scientific and philosophical production to the cultural dimension.

As an answer to the consequences of the fall, the Dutch neo-Calvinist tradition points to a comprehensive redemption in Jesus Christ. It would include the cultural sphere as well as every human enterprise that involves creativity. Besides, given that culture is understood as a good thing within creation, it is both a gift and a task to be attained. To Carvalho,

> [...] human culture as a whole is also part of God's creational order. Many of its aspects (state, family, economy, morality, etc.) already existed before the church and continue to be valid with the coming kingdom of God. New creation does not imply the destruction or the dissolution of the original creational order; it is not subversion, but the restoration and glorification of creation's original architecture.[36]

Grounded in a neo-Calvinist worldview, many ministries within Christianity have been developed. One example that could be mentioned for applying principles derived from the Dutch tradition through its *modus vivendi* is *L'Abri Fellowship*.[37] Founded in 1955 in Switzerland by Francis and Edith Schaeffer, L'Abri was deeply influenced by the ideas of the Dooyeweerdian art historian Hans Rookmaaker.[38] One of the features of this ministry is the integration of

---

36. Carvalho, 2009, 73.
37. For an overview of the beginnings of L'Abri, see Edith Schaeffer, *L'Abri* (Crossway Books, Wheaton, USA, 1992).
38. Hans Rookmaaker (1922-1977) was for many years an art history Professor at the Free University of Amsterdam, where he applied neo-Calvinism to the arts. A few years later Rookmaaker founded the Dutch

different aspects of life under the Lordship of Christ. According to Steve Turner, a former L'Abri student in the 70s in Switzerland,

> Life at L'Abri sharpened our perceptions. Many of us had come from backgrounds which encouraged us to categorize all culture as either Christian or non-Christian, spiritual or fleshy. Schaeffer, influenced by the Dutch art historian Hans Rookmaaker, instead proposed that we should look at works individually. Rather than asking, is this artist saved? Ask, Is this piece of work technically excellent? Is it a valid expression of the artist's view of the world? Are form and content well integrated? Is truth communicated?[39]

The reference to L'Abri and to Francis Schaeffer is important because his work has become well known in the evangelical realm in Brazil, as new editions of some of his main books have been released. Such a fact may explain, partially at least, the increasing interest in the reformational tradition in the Brazilian context, especially in reference to Hans Rookmaaker and Herman Dooyeweerd. In 2010, Rookmaaker's book *Art Needs No Justification* was translated and published in Portuguese, and in 2012 the same publisher released a biography written by Laurel Gasque entitled *Rookmaaker: Arts and the Christian Mind*. The connection between reformational thinking and L'Abri has become clearer in recent years in Brazil, when L'Abri workers Guilherme de Carvalho and Rodolfo Amorim translated – in addition to articles and chapters in books – Dooyeweerd's *In the Twilight of Western Thought*. Dooyeweerd's book about the state – *Estado e Soberania* in Portuguese – was published in 2014 and *The Roots of Western Culture* in 2015. In the same year, *The Contours of a*

---

branch of L'Abri Fellowship, which exists to this day. See Colin Duriez, *Francis Schaeffer: An authentic life* (IVP, Nottingham, UK, 2008).

39. Steve Turner, *Imagine: A vision for Christians in the arts* (Illinois, InterVarsity Press, 2001), 11.

Christian Philosophy by Kalsbeeck – an introduction to cosmonomic philosophy – was translated and published as well.

It is also worth noticing the recent development and establishment of the Brazilian version of *Christians in Science, Associação Brasileira de Cristãos na Ciência,* which was developed as an initiative of the *Kuyper Association for Transdisciplinary Studies* (Associação Kuyper para Estudos Transdisciplinares, or AKET) and supported by the *John Templeton Foundation.* It came to bridge a gap within Christian communities in Brazil by relating all areas of life to the Christian faith.

Thus, recent publications, the development of associations such as the one mentioned above, communities of Christian thinkers as well as Christian artists, a view of Christians as culture's reformers, has started to gain strength in the Brazilian context. There are a lot of challenges yet to be faced, though the first fruits of reformational thinking can already be seen in culture, and it stands as a powerful and meaningful response to the question raised in the beginning regarding the relation of Christians and the world.

6

A DIALOGUE BETWEEN AMSTERDAM, LAUSANNE AND MEDELLÍN:

A Reformational Critique of Latin American Theology

As REFORMATIONAL THINKING gains momentum, especially in Brazil, it is inevitable that it will need to be in dialogue with the theological perspectives present in Latin America. From the first meeting on biblical worldview and integral transformation,[1] that took place in 2005

---
1. This was a gathering of evangelical pastors, theologians and lay Christians working in various fields, who had had some contact with the reformational tradition.

in Curitiba, a systematic reflection was initiated on important issues to the church and to the Brazilian society as a whole, based on the Kuyperian tradition of thought.

However, it is still too early to speak of a proper dialogue with other perspectives, since the first efforts of the authors who share this tradition has been primarily to point out similarities and differences with what has already been produced, in terms of a Christian reflection, especially from the perspective of the *Theology of Missão Integral (TMI)*[2] and *Liberation Theology* (LT) in recognition of the legacy of these movements. Guilherme de Carvalho, one of the articulators of reformational thought in Brazil states that:

> The idea that the Christian worldview should have a decisive impact on all areas of life, including thought, developed in Dutch neo-Calvinism, has its parallel in Christian movements such as European Christian socialism, liberation theology and the theology of *missão integral*, reflected in the Lausanne Covenant.[3]

The presentation of *Theology of Missão Integral* (TMI) and Liberation Theology (LT), intends to highlight the points of congruency and tension with a cosmonomic perspective of thought and praxis, presenting a critique of them using Dooyeweerd's philosophy. The description of these theological proposals in a panoramic way does not represent all their theoretical and practical strength in different fields. So, it serves more as an initial conversation between traditions, and less as a detailed comparative study of these important theological perspectives.

---

2. A literal translation would be *Integral Mission*, but the Portuguese form will be kept here.
3. Guilherme de Carvalho, *Cosmovisão cristã e transformação*, 123.

A DIALOGUE BETWEEN AMSTERDAM, LAUSANNE AND MEDELLÍN

6.1 Theology of Missão Integral (TMI)

As LT could be called a contextual theology as it turned to the questions of the Latin American context, in response to the *Second Vatican Council* (1962-1965), the TMI was born as a response given by Latin American Protestants to the issues discussed at the *First International Congress on World Evangelization* held in Lausanne, Switzerland, in 1974.

The main articulators of this proposal in the 1970s were: René Padilha, Pedro Savage, Samuel Escobar, Pedro Arana, Emilio Nuñez and Valdir Steuernagel. For José Miguez Bonino, although the movement has had influence on evangelical groups in the US and the evangelical wing of the Anglican Church in England, the movement of *Missão Integral* "[...] has its own face and a particular story in our continent [Latin America]."[4]

The Congress on World Evangelization, which brought together Protestant Christians from around the world, aimed to reflect on the significance of the church's mission in the second half of the twentieth century. The major theme of this theological movement was: *The whole gospel to the whole person*, in the sense of recovering a non-dualistic view of the human being and reality. Thus, the gospel and salvation would not only concern the salvation of the soul, but would be a transforming power of reality, including social dynamics.

According to Ricardo Gondim,

> [...] There was a clear effervescence among Latin Americans who demanded greater freedom to "contextualize" theology. With less tutelage from the North American headquarters, churches and seminaries saw in the *Missão Integral* the possibility of carrying out a mission along the lines proposed by the Lausanne Covenant.[5]

---

4. José Miguez Bonino, *Rostos do protestantismo latino-americano*, 49.
5. Ricardo Gondim, *Missão integral: em busca de uma identidade evangéli-*

At the heart of the discussions was contained a double critique: towards that of *theological fundamentalism* as well as that of *theological liberalism*. About this, Bonino states that:

> The movement begins with an affirmation of the *centrality of Scripture,* on the double front of the critique of clumsy literalism and the arbitrary interpretation of fundamentalism and a liberalism that seemed to reduce the Bible to a collection of documents from the past or to a repository of religious truths and general and universal ethics.[6]

The realization of a low influence of Protestantism in Latin America, in the face of a reality of poverty and social exclusion, made the proponents of TMI, in which its institutional expression is found in entities such as the Latin American Theological Fraternity (*Fraternidade Teológica Latino-Americana* - FTL), seek to articulate the holistic dimension of the gospel, focusing both on salvation and on the social transformation of communities. In this sense, it was stated that "[...] any evangelization that just wants to save souls impoverishes the gospel, has a unilateral doctrine of salvation and does not dignify the human being as created by God in his image."[7]

From the perspective of TMI, therefore, there is a recognition of the human being as a cultural and social being, whose expectations and needs can and should be answered by the evangelical action, which needs to see the human being in his totality, beyond the soul. Likewise, there is a concern with the structural dimensions of society, such as politics and the economy. A comprehensive Christian action in the world could not fail to take these aspects into consideration.

---

ca (São Paulo: Fonte Editorial, 2010), 61.
6. José Miguez Bonino, *Rostos do protestantismo latino-americano*, 49.
7. Steuernagel, Valdir *apud* Ricardo Gondim, *Missão integral*, 62.

The expression "the whole Gospel" meant for TMI not only the proclamation of the contents of the Christian message for individuals, but a cosmic message that would reveal a God who "embraces the whole world" and does not address the individual *per se*, [not making a] distinction of gender, culture or ethnicity and economical condition.[8]

In this way, TMI represents an evangelical Latin American proposal for Christian social action in the world. Thus, it can be framed as a contextual theology, given that it dialogues with particular aspects of the Brazilian and Latin American context, without giving up a Christian view of reality.

Considering the political dimension, the movement had references in the Anglican Bishop Robinson Cavalcanti – who until his death in 2012, had a strong influence on the production of TMI and in the English sociologist based in Brazil, Paul Freston. Historically, Cavalcanti was one of the founders, in 1990, of MEP (trans. "Evangelical Progressive Movement"), in which its perspective and work differed profoundly from the traditional identification of evangelicals with the political right and with more conservative views. Carvalho observes that:

> The movement started to gain visibility in the 1989 presidential election, when the evangelical Pro-Lula movement was organized, led by Robinson Cavalcanti, which even appeared on television during the first round, causing an impact among evangelicals, who tended to demonize the left.[9]

One of the key themes emphasized by TMI is the notion of *social justice*, which makes their adherents gravitate less around conservatism. In similarity to Liberation Theology, there is an emphasis on

---

8. Ricardo Gondim, *Missão integral*, 68.
9. Guilherme de Carvalho, *Cosmovisão cristã e transformação*, 241.

the present condition of poverty in Latin America and in the struggle to transform this condition that oppresses human beings. The Christian's role, according to their proponents would be a critical political engagement.

This defence of social justice, understood through the lenses of contemporary social theories, makes the movement flirt with a more socialist political orientation, sometimes assimilating some interpretative categories, such as the *dependency theory* and *historical materialism*, which could be questioned from a Christian standpoint.

The critical point for neo-Calvinists is not the dialogue with these matrices of thought, but their uncritical reception and the lack of a Christian hermeneutic filter, insofar as some political and economic theses are incorporated in certain anthropologies and theologies, which would be incompatible with a Christian worldview.

Neo-Calvinists recognize, however, that *Missão Integral*'s predilection for the left may be more a momentary strategy than an ideological commitment.[10] Such an alignment would be configured as a *co-belligerence* against a common enemy: in this case, social injustice. It can be inferred that this perspective is close to the position of the Kuyperian-Dooyeweerdian tradition of affirming what promotes the sovereignty of God and the consequent promotion of the full function of each sphere of sovereignty. Insofar as the role of the State is to promote justice, any initiative in this direction – even if it is of non-Christians – must be supported and encouraged.

6.1.1 Similarities and Tensions between TMI and Neo-Calvinism

Borrowing from the Dooyeweerdian conceptual language, it can be said that the primordial ground-motive on which the political theology of TMI builds its action is the same that is present in the

---

10. *Ibid.*, 251.

neo-Calvinist worldview. Both perspectives share the fundamental belief of a creation-fall-redemption, also including the eschatological principle of the consummation. Another common feature is an emphasis on the Lordship of Christ over all of life. In this sense, the Jarabacoa statement reads:

> We reaffirm our firm conviction of faith in the Holy Scriptures, and, within the tradition of the Reformation, we proclaim Christ's lordship over the individual and over his church. With the same strength, we confess that He is the Lord of all created reality. We believe that Christ's redemptive and renewing power affects not only the individual, but also the social, economic, cultural and political sphere in which he is present.[11]

According to Carvalho, these themes presented in the Jarabacoa Declaration (1983),[12] have "[...] evangelical precision and coherence, [since] it avoids indicating a specific political ideology."[13] In the same way, such a statement, while encouraging Christian action in all creational structures, does not ignore the presence of sin as a distortion of a correct orientation of the human religious centre. This approach avoids a fruitless isolation, as in Christians against politics, for example, or an acritical reception of certain models of political action.

Drawing from the ideas of the philosopher Nicholas Wolterstorff, Brazilian reformationals defend an evangelical political action

---

11. Jarabacoa Declaration. Available in: <http://www.ftl.org.br/new/downloads/bt02.pdf>.
12. Such a declaration was the outcome of a meeting of theologians and Christians in politics, who were called by Fraternidade Teológica Latino-Americana (Latin American Theological Fraternity), that took place in 1983 in the city of Jarabacoa, in the Dominican Republic, aiming to reflect on the themes of Christians and political action.
13. Guilherme de Carvalho, *Cosmovisão cristã e transformação*, 260.

of a *formative* nature, whose vision is that of "[...] earthly existence as the *locus* of a intramundane religious experience [...]",[14] as opposed to an *avertive* action, in which its emphasis would be on an extra-worldly form of religiosity. The *formative* perspective would aim at a constant reform of the political and social structures, in a kind of application of the principle *Ecclesia Reformata Semper Reformanda Est* to the political field.

In this direction, there is a *progressivism* that brings together the different movements based on TMI with the reformed Dutch tradition. However, neo-Calvinists reject the humanist type of progressivism, which interprets the social order as mere social construction, as developed in the idea of the *social contract*, by French Enlightenment philosophers. The social order would be, in contrast, the result of a divine order rooted in creation, and not based on abstract rational principles or specific historical aspects.[15]

One of the central criticisms of Carvalho toward TMI comes from an alleged lack of understanding the social order in connection with the created order. Furthermore, the theologian asks: "After all, *what progressivism does* TMI speak of?"[16]

Still following Wolterstorff, Carvalho affirms that a *reformational progressivism* constitutes:

> [a] *cosmoformative* [...] Christianity (*world-formative*) not [...] merely disruptive, but redemptive; and not reactionary, as it understands that there is a line of advancement and cultural differentiation rooted in the cultural mandate in Genesis. The neo-Calvinist form of progressivism would then be the commitment to the *reform* of the social order, to

---

14. Guilherme de Carvalho, *Cosmovisão cristã e transformação*, 261.
15. *Raízes da cultura ocidental*, 72.
16. Guilherme de Carvalho, *Cosmovisão cristã e transformação*, 262.

submit it to the laws of God.[17]

What is at stake for the neo-Calvinists is the proposal of a Christian political philosophy. As already commented, the Dooyeweerdian project foresees an epistemological rearrangement, proposing a new way of interpreting the relations between the sciences and the different forms of knowledge. In a sense, this is an audacious project of reforming thinking. Such an undertaking is equally extended to the sphere of political activity.

For the defenders of these ideas in Brazil, the Kuyperian-Dooyeweerdian proposal of philosophy and politics is consistent with the ground-motive of creation, fall and redemption. At this point, they intend to collaborate with the reflection of TMI, which would lack an innovative proposal, rooted in the philosophical Christian categories. Reformationals see the rapprochement between Christians and the political left, for example, with suspicion, since their social philosophies are built on apostate religious ground motives.

However, this criticism of socialism does not cause immediate uncritical acceptance of the principles of conservatism or of the classic political right. Leonardo Ramos – Brazilian author who is part of AKET (Kuyper Association for Transdisciplinary Studies) – defends the overcoming of the *right/left* binomial, not so much through a *centrism* or by a balance between the two poles, but by adopting a "[...] posture more to the 'right' than the right and more to the 'left' than the left, more 'traditional' than the traditional and more 'revolutionary' than the revolutionaries."[18] Therefore, the attitude of Christians to this binomial should be one of distrust, insofar as

---

17. *Ibid.*, 263.
18. Leonardo Ramos, "Os ídolos do nosso tempo: A cosmovisão cristã em um mundo de esquerdas e direitas." In: Rodolfo Amorim, Marcel Camargo e Leonardo Ramos (Org.), *Fé cristã e cultura contemporânea*, 147.

[these] two extremes: *individualist*: pro-market, politically right-wing; and *collectivist*: in general, pro-state, politically on the left [...] reify modern metanarratives – market and state, Liberalism and Marxism –, which in turn are idols of our time and, as such, lead to idolatry and alienation of God's purposes.[19]

Another point of tension between the neo-Calvinists and the TMI concerns the extra-ecclesiastical *Christian action*, that is, the place and mission of the church in relation to the place and mission of para-ecclesiastical institutions. Carvalho's criticism of TMI's perspective is that it often does not give these institutions their own legitimacy, making them extensions of the church's mission. In other words, they would only have legitimacy wherever the church is absent. There is still, according to him, leaders and ministers who see any social project as the responsibility of the government.[20]

In contrast,

This problem simply does not exist in neo-Calvinist thinking, because in it the involvement of believers in para-church and extra-church projects is not seen as a way to "compensate" for the weakness of the church, but as one of its main purposes. In this perspective, the church is seen as a kind of "pastoral centre", which aims to train and send the saints to actions of integral transformation in the various fields of society.[21]

In view of the presentation of the elements of the reformational tradition, it is clear that there is an encouragement of the occupation of spaces (spheres) by Christians, as a way of promoting the lordship of Christ over the whole of reality. There is no combat of distortions via absence or an ecclesiastical centralization, but a fulfilment, which

---

19. *Ibid.*, 146.
20. See Guilherme de Carvalho, *Cosmovisão cristã e transformação*, 269.
21. *Ibid.*, 270.

sees in each particular sphere a *locus* of manifestation of divine sovereignty and glory.

Certainly, there are more points of approximation rather than of tension between these two traditions. It is up to Christians, from both sides, to continue a fruitful dialogue that can serve as a reference for the construction of edifying paradigms of a Christian engagement that is relevant and that makes a difference in various fields.

6.2 Liberation Theology

As in the case of TMI, Liberation Theology (LT) has an extensive literature and a range of authors who deal with the most varied subjects. Its influence and importance in Latin America transcend the ecclesiastical level – both Catholic and Protestant – being recognized as an important theological tradition by authors from different fields. Furthermore, many liberation theologians were engaged in political struggles, especially against dictatorial regimes in Latin America in the second half of the twentieth century. It is important to emphasize, again, that the scope of this section will be to outline the fundamental features of LT as well as presenting a brief critique from a reformational standpoint, though not in an exhaustive and detailed way, an undertaking that would require a specific work.

From the great universal theological treatises to contextual theologies: this was the path taken by many theologians and theologies, especially in the 20th century. These theologies arise from the demands of minorities,[22] who were generally excluded, in some aspect, be it social, political, economic or, more recently, gender. Therefore, the first statement that is made is that LT is a contextual theology, whose articulation takes place in the experience of a specific subject. And what experience and subject are these? In the case of Latin America, it is the experience of *exclusion,* and the subject

---

22. Or majorities, as in the case of the poor in Latin America.

are the *poor*. The theological articulation would be, first, a struggle for *emancipation* and then for *liberation*.[23]

According to Alessandro Rocha, "[...] LT emerges from the articulation between the positivity of faith and the historical reality of the poor."[24] Such articulation would have started as the response of Latin American theologians to the Second Vatican Council (1962-1965), which was responsible for a greater opening of the Roman Catholic Church in contextual themes. In that sense, "[this event] was important to work on an ecclesiology that understood the Church as the people of God."[25] In a way, since the Council, there has been an opening for a decentralization of ecclesiastical structures and a consequent appreciation of the particular demands of specific contexts.

An important event that followed the Second Vatican Council was the *Conferência do Episcopado Latino-Americano* (Latin American Episcopal Conference) held in Medellín, Colombia, in 1968. In it, «[...] arises with great strength a consciousness of solidarity with the poor that articulates two dimensions of the Latin American reality that until then had little dialogue in theological reflection: historical unity and political dimension of the faith."[26] This dimension of historicity, related to the *praxis*, of all theology is one of the hallmarks of LT.

> The origin of LT in Latin America is not accidental: a reflection on the faith based on the concerns of the popular sectors that suffer injustice could hardly have been born in the rich countries of the world. In rich countries, concerns are different: secularization, the abundance that

---

23. Rosino Gibellini, *A teologia do século XX*, 349.
24. Alessandro Rodrigues Rocha, "Teologia da libertação." In: Fernando Bortolleto Filho et al. (Org.), *Dicionário brasileiro de teologia*, 962-65.
25. *Ibid.*, 962.
26. *Ibid.*, 963.

produces materialism and atheism, the loss of the meaning of life and the fear of war. In the third world the concerns are: how to survive, how to get rid of injustice, how to get out of the situation of hunger and misery in which the majority lives, how to liberate ourselves.[27]

The pioneers' authors of LT in Latin America were Gustavo Gutierrez, Juan Luis Segundo, Hugo Assmann, José Comblin, Enrique Dussel, José Miguéz Bonino, Rubem Alves and Leonardo Boff. The book *Theology of Liberation* by Gustavo Gutiérrez, published in 1971 was fundamental to lay the foundations of liberation theology. In it, "[it is sought] to reconcile salvation with the historical process of liberation."[28]

In the theological labour of the liberation struggle, its articulators identified three moments that reveal the foundations of LT. The method is composed by three moments: *to see, to judge* and *to act*. Its aim is to articulate theology with the liberation of the oppressed. The first moment – to *see* - concerns an understanding of the situation of the poor, at a pre-theological stage, which goes beyond an individual analysis, touching the *social structures* of oppression. In order to *see* the real situation of the poor, liberation theology opts for the sociological tools of interpretation, a Mediação Socioanalítica (MSA) – a *Socio-analytical Mediation* (SAM).

Regarding the choice of this method, Carvalho observes that, "[...] in the selection of which SAM is better suited to the cause of the poor, the theologian will use theological criteria to identify which one best favours the poor; it will also reject those aspects of SAM that are destructive to the faith."[29] The sociological lens tends to be of

---

27. Victor Codina, *¿Que es la Teologia de la Liberacion?* (Santiago: Rehue, 1987), 13.
28. Alessandro Rodrigues Rocha, "Teologia da libertação." In: Fernando Bortolleto Filho et al. (Org.), *Dicionário brasileiro de teologia*, 963.
29. Guilherme de Carvalho, *Cosmovisão cristã e transformação*, 144.

Marxist orientation, the use of which is the biggest point of criticism of LT. However, according to Alessandro Rocha, "[...] the humanist Marx is taken and not the dogmatic, economist or materialist. Marx is taken as a social critic, but the values are those of faith."[30]

The authors of LT acknowledge these criticisms and respond to them by arguing that no theology is neutral – a point in common with the Dooyeweerdian perspective – and that all theological practice implies an interpretation of reality. Codina defends the use of the social sciences as an analytical tool but reinforces that the ultimate foundation of LT is in the Word of God and not in sociology. He says, however, that "[LT] cannot fail to analyze reality, something that other theologies also do, even though they are often not aware of it."[31]

The second moment, *to judge* is configured as the theological labour itself. This is the moment to "[...] ask about what the word of God says about such an analyzed reality."[32] This would be the prophetic attitude of *denunciation, announcement and transformation*, illuminated by the Scriptures.[33] In this context, practices such as popular reading of the Bible are encouraged, as the divine revelation embodied in history speaks directly to an excluded subject in a given context. In this sense, some contemporary liberation theologians have identified the figure of the excluded in different perspectives: black, woman, indigenous, gay, transgender, etc.

Finally, the third moment, *to act*, gives the militant and activist character of social and political engagement of LT. It wants to

---

30. Alessandro Rodrigues Rocha, "Teologia da libertação." In: Fernando Bortolleto Filho et al. (Org.), *Dicionário brasileiro de teologia*, 964.
31. Victor Codina, *¿Que es la Teologia de la Liberacion?*, 25.
32. Alessandro Rodrigues Rocha, "Teologia da libertação." In: Fernando Bortolleto Filho et al. (Org.), *Dicionário brasileiro de teologia*, 964.
33. Victor Codina, *¿Que es la Teologia de la Liberacion?*, 28.

see liberation, and not just in the theoretical dimension of reflection. "It is not enough to have correct ideas, you have to put them into practice."[34] And this practice is seen as a clear option for the poor and the oppressed. In this direction, the theological labour involves the recognition that this doing is situated in a certain *praxis*, and that for theology there is no option of neutrality.

6.2.1 The Reformational Critique of Liberation Theology

The reformational authors recognize the importance and the biblical coherence of the emphasis placed on the poor by LT. It is precisely on this issue, recognizes Carvalho, that the Dutch tradition, in its contextualization to Brazil, is subject to criticism, since "[...] the problem of poverty, economic exploitation and the theme of liberation are absent in Dooyeweerd."[35] Indeed, following the logic of intellectual production connected to a context, it is notable that the issues with which Dooyeweerd dealt had to do more with a spiritual crisis – given the period of post-war in Europe – than to a material crisis. In defence of the reformational tradition, the Brazilian theologian states, however, that "[...] one cannot deduce from this absence an incompatibility with the themes of poverty and liberation, especially because these themes are native to the Christian worldview."[36]

The points of tension, nonetheless, between liberation theology and the Kuyperian-Dooyeweerdian proposal are much more explicit than the previous relationship with TMI. The main criticisms presented by neo-Calvinists, which have implications in different dimensions of human experience and for the church in Latin America and Brazil, are concerning the dualism that *nature and grace* presents in liberation theology; a concept of *praxis* that leads to *histor-*

---

34. *Ibid.*, 29.
35. Guilherme de Carvalho, *Cosmovisão cristã e transformação*, 263.
36. *Ibid.*, 264.

icism; and the problem of the Socio-Analytical Mediation (SAM).

6.3 The Dualism of Nature and Grace

As already mentioned in this reflection, Dooyeweerd interprets this dualism *nature and grace* as a religious *ground-motive*, that was a result of the synthesis of the creation-fall-redemption *ground-motive* with the Greek *matter and form*. Starting from a flawed understanding of the fall, this dualism propagates the idea that human rationality would not have been affected by sin. Therefore, it would be possible to constitute a neutral science, capable of analyzing reality and of unveiling the real.

"In building [...] its proposal of liberation, TL uses the Thomist scheme of the relationship between faith and rationality",[37] says Carvalho. The author continues with his criticism, stating that in the liberation practice of LT "[...] it is assumed that faith must be supported [...] by a conception of rationality and theoretical thought prior to itself in order to constitute as a scientific discourse."[38] The great novelty of LT is the use of the young science, sociology, and no longer the philosophical tools of other times. Codina himself recognizes this tradition when he states that:

> On the question of using human and social sciences to judge reality, it must be said that social sciences that are more serious, objective and able to better understand reality should be used. [...] This is what the Church has been doing through the centuries, using philosophical or scientific elements that are alien to the faith for its theology. This is the case of the early Church with [...] Plato, what Saint Thomas did with Aristotle's philosophy, what modern moral theology did by distinguishing in Freud's psychology the scientific elements of the atheist

---

37. *Ibid.*, 149.
38. *Ibid.*, 149.

philosophy of the author of psychoanalysis [...].[39]

Thus, starting from Dooyeweerd, it is possible to say that the dogma of the religious autonomy of reason is in operation in LT, as it seeks to interpret reality from a free and autonomous science, which, based on objectivity is the instrument to see what is happening. For Carvalho,

> [...] Christian faith and theology ("grace") are accommodated to a socialist interpretation of "nature", so that the very concept of "salvation" is adapted to a Marxist-based anthropological conception. In effect, therefore, the *vision of social wholeness* used by LT is socialism, a specific form of secular humanism.[40]

Similarly, there is a tendency in LT of blaming an oppressive system, as the main if not the sole cause for the condition of the poor, which shadows the role of the individual in this process. Therefore, the language of *worldview* is absent, since the role of the individual is seen as secondary in the process of liberation. In this sense, the only viable path would be revolution – the radical transformation of structures – as opposed to the neo-Calvinist ideal of reformation.

For Brazilian neo-Calvinist authors, LT tends to conceive reality as being socially constructed, without references to a creational order. To reinforce this point, Carvalho says that "[...] libertarian Bible readings (feminist theology and some forms of contextual theology, for example) suffer almost universally of an insensitivity to normative structures for social life."[41]

The nature and grace dualism affects the entire theological con-

---

39. Victor Codina, *¿Que es la Teologia de la Liberacion?*, 25-26.
40. Guilherme de Carvalho, *Cosmovisão cristã e transformação*, 150.
41. Guilherme de Carvalho, "O senhorio de Cristo e a missão da igreja na cultura." In: Leonardo Ramos et al. (Org.), *Fé cristã e cultura contemporânea*, 70.

struction of LT, being responsible, in the same way, for an understanding of the *praxis* that ends up absolutizing the historical aspect of reality.

6.4 The Problem of Praxis and Historicism

In general, *praxis* can be defined as a complex engendering between reflection (theory) and action (practice), encompassing the whole of human life. In LT, there is a differentiation and questioning in relation to two different types of *praxis*: *theoretical* and *historical*. According to Carvalho, there is in authors like Bonino and Segundo – and in this tradition as a whole – an appreciation of *historical praxis*, as that which conditions any theoretical production, including theology. That is why one of the problems of theology concerns its relationship with the *praxis*.[42]

In that direction,

> Praxis shapes theology by asking questions for theology, and theology assesses and criticizes the faith that moves action, but the theory itself does not engender praxis, nor can it be controlled, being just a moment of contemplation that it is born of life and returns to it.[43]

This conception differs from the neo-Calvinist interpretation since there is no ontological primacy of one type of praxis over the other. For neo-Calvinists, this perspective present in LT absolutizes one aspect of human experience, in this case the *historical* one, tending to reduce all other aspects to it, generating a particular form of *historicism*.

The problem lies in the fact that the historical aspect is always relative, since it has no universalizing basis; it is always particular and contextual. However, the *liberation* would be the evaluative

---
42. Guilherme de Carvalho, *Cosmovisão cristã e transformação*, 146.
43. *Ibid.*, 147.

parameter of the historical development in the understanding of LT. Thus, neo-Calvinists see a risk of relativizing – via historical conditioning – the contents of the faith and the authority of the Scriptures, in a kind of overestimation of *orthopraxis*, to the detriment of *orthodoxy*.[44]

Carvalho mentions the reflection of the reformed philosopher James Olthuis on the work of José Luis Segundo, which demonstrates how Segundo would have formulated his theological system based on an *evolutionary* concept of reality, coming from the theologian and anthropologist Teilhard de Chardin. According to Olthuis, Segundo interprets history as an ascending dialectic dynamic towards liberation. From that,

> At each stage of this evolutionary process, human "truths" are transformed, as Segundo explicitly says: "there are no universal truths in the process of liberation; the only truth is liberation itself." In other words, for him, the *liberation praxis is the only truth*.[45]

Therefore, by means of the absolutization of a relative aspect, this Latin American tradition would be subject to synthesize the Christian faith with certain elements that would distort it, putting it at risk of losing the true transformative potential of the gospel, insofar as it flirts with humanist and libertarian conceptions of humanity and of reality.

6.5 The Socio-Analytical Mediation (SAM)

For LT, every praxis has an ideology that supports it and that ends up influencing any human production. This ideology would be of a pre-theological character; therefore, it would need a sociological apparatus for its interpretation. In this way, the process of *seeing* would

---

44. Guilherme de Carvalho, *Cosmovisão cristã e transformação*, 148.
45. *Ibid.*, 148.

be the responsibility of the social sciences whereas, in a second step, *judging* would be the responsibility of theology.

The critique articulated at this point is that LT seems to postulate that only sociology would be able to see the *real condition* of oppression and the oppressed. This would only be possible insofar as "[...] faith is assumed to be a gift of grace *superimposed on nature*, in such a way that the gaze of faith is not part of reality, coming *after the sociological gaze*."[46]

For the reformational tradition, the condition of the poor is not only sociological, but has several aspects that this SAM cannot account for: biotic-ecological, ethical, pystic, and so on. The disagreement between the two traditions is evident in the fact that, for neo-Calvinists, faith is an anthropological element, rooted in human nature, and not a gift purely superimposed on nature.

Therefore, "[...] *there is not and cannot be a socio-analytical 'mediation' for theology*, but rather a scientific *cooperation* between the social sciences and the sciences of faith in the search for understanding the real and complex situation of the oppressed."[47] The risk taken by LT is of a sociological narrowing that identifies Christ's redemption as mere social transformation. The scope of redemption, in its entirety, transforms all aspects of the created reality, renewing the human being into a new anthropology, starting from the new creation.

Likewise, the conception of this SAM is criticized by accepting uncritically a neutral science capable of interpreting – without assumptions – the created reality. As already explained in the course of this work from a Dooyeweerdian perspective, to give such *status* to sociology would be to insist and to perpetuate the *dogma of religious autonomy of reason*.

---

46. *Ibid.*, 155.
47. *Ibid.*, 155.

Thus, regarding theological debates with political and social implications, the Brazilian context has two robust traditions of thought: *Teologia da Missão Integral* and Liberation Theology. The Kuyperian/Dooyeweerdian tradition has points in common with these traditions, but also points of tension and criticism in relation to the theological and philosophical foundations of these movements.

However, in the face of a still incipient scenario of debate and dialogue, it would be presumptuous to have a prognosis. What can be stated is that an open conversation between these traditions can contribute to the flourishing of God's kingdom in Latin America.

7

FINAL CONSIDERATIONS

AFTER DEALING THE MAIN ELEMENTS of Herman Dooyeweerd's Reformational philosophy, I noted that the Dutch thinker produced his reflection in the context of a theological movement whose scope was very comprehensive, namely, neo-Calvinism. The premise on which the members of the movement, especially Abraham Kuyper, developed their actions was the understanding of Christianity as an integral (holistic) worldview. This is to say that they believed there was no area of human life that was not under the lordship of Christ. Dooyeweerd's greatest insight was to apply this principle to theoretical thinking.

For the authors of this tradition, speaking of a private faith and religion, which are not in dialogue with different fields of human life, is something inconceivable, that goes against the nature of belief and Christian faith. The Amsterdam philosopher is therefore suspicious of any theoretical construction that alienates the pistic aspect from other dimensions of our existence.

Another element discussed here was the understanding of religion as the orientation of the heart – the religious centre of life – towards an absolute: a source of ultimate meaning, which contains an explanation of the origin of all things, something from which everything else depends – *arché*. This conception differs significantly from the image of religion constructed in modernity. I observed throughout the book that religion, in the modern period, has tended to be reduced to a private belief. This fact, according to Dooyeweerd, finds roots in a distorted model of rationality, which tends to disregard the religious aspect in its theoretical construction.

For the Dutch author, this distorted construction of theoretical thought is expressed in the *dogma of the religious autonomy of reason*. Such dogma asserts that rationality is free from religious influence in its field of investigation. Dooyeweerd challenges this perspective, stating that, contrary to what Kant imagined, theoretical thought always has a pre-theoretical presupposition, which is based on a religious choice.

This Dooyeweerdian opening to a new conception of religion and, consequently, of a new model of relationship between faith and rationality can serve as a reference for the reformation and transformation of certain instances of public debate and scientific and philosophical development that are still closed to these dimensions. In many circles, the dogma of the religious autonomy of reason seems to go unchallenged.

Furthermore, we saw that the philosophical contribution of Herman Dooyeweerd sheds light on the relationship between philosophy and Christianity. Such a relationship has always been a controversial point in the history of Christianity. The Dutch philosopher understands that Christianity contains a fundamental religious motive that is radically different from all the others. According to him, at the heart of the Christian faith there is the fundamental idea of creation, fall and redemption as an absolute narrative for human life. For the reformational thinker, this ground-motive is an indissoluble antithesis, operating in the human heart at a pre-theoretical level. Any attempt to synthesize it with other principles gives rise to apostate ground-motives. Thus, an honest dialogue between different traditions of thought would involve a disclosure of these ground-motives at work in the human heart.

A theme that was already central to the sixteenth century reformers was identified in reformational philosophy as well: the fact that the knowledge of God and of the self go together. The ego, in Dooyeweerd, is thought of as the *locus* of the *imago Dei*, a defining characteristic of human beings, which distinguishes them from the rest of created reality. The Dooyeweerdian self does not have content in itself, since it is constituted by its relationships, the main one being the relationship with its origin, source of all meaning. The self is transcendental in that it cannot be reduced to any aspect of temporal reality.

In this direction, the inevitable question that we tried to face was the one regarding the subordination of philosophy to theology. Given that Dooyeweerd sees Christ as the true *arché* - the ultimate revelation of who God is and who human beings are – would not Christian theology be the most qualified science to undertake any project of knowledge? The Dooyeweerdian answer was no. The proper object of theology is not the biblical ground-motive itself, but the faith aspect of created order. Thus, theology is also subordinate to the religious operation of the ground-motive in the heart. It does not have a privileged place in understanding reality and the human being.

Similarly, a brief reflection was made about the postmodern theses of philosophical interpretation. We saw that Dooyeweerd does not see the contemporary period as a radical break with modernity. In this sense, he departs from the dominant interpretation. According to the Amsterdam author, what is seen is an emphasis on the pole of freedom, since the ground-motive at work is the humanist nature/freedom. While modernity emphasized science, objectivity and structural determination over individual will, contemporaries tend to value what he called the ideal of personality. Since this is a dualistic ground-motive, it is not possible to transcend this dialectical polarity.

In addition to theoretical contributions to philosophy, he paid special attention to cultural dynamics in distinct contexts. I developed a brief reflection using Dooyeweerd analytical categories to discuss the cultural field and the field of political theology, noticeably, in the Latin American and Brazilian contexts.

We conclude by stating that the present work is an introduction to the thought of Herman Dooyeweerd. His philosophical legacy has already been explored in different fields of knowledge. Discussing each of them would require different projects. Certainly, it is up to each author, in their own field, to use the theoretical tools available in Dooyeweerd as instruments for the development of new theories and, hopefully, for a Christian reformation of the mind.

The ideas discussed here can be further developed in dialogue with different traditions of thought. The Dooyeweerdian perspective serves as an encouragement to all Christians to exercise their vocation in different fields, having the conviction of Christ's sovereignty over all reality.

Soli Deo Gloria

ABOUT THE AUTHOR

Josué Reichow was born in Pelotas, Rio Grande do Sul, the southernmost state in Brazil. There he did his studies in the Social Sciences, with a particular interest in Sociology, and contemporary themes in social theory, with a specialization in modernity/postmodernity and critical theory. As a Christian he started to ask questions about his faith, both in the academic setting as well as in the broader public sense. Encouraged by a friend, he visited the L'Abri community in Brazil, where he was introduced to the reformational tradition. Between 2012 and 2014, Josué studied Philosophy (at *Unisinos*, a Jesuit University) and Theology (at *Faculdades EST*, a Lutheran School of Theology), where he studied the philosophy of Herman Dooyeweerd and his reception in the Brazilian context. He has taught theology, philosophy, and worldview in Theological Seminaries, and Sociology, Philosophy, and Religious Studies for High School students at *Colégio Sinodal* in the city of São Leopoldo.

In 2016 Josué moved to the UK with his wife Lili to join the work of L'Abri, welcoming people from all over the world, cooking meals, gardening, facilitating discussions, and lecturing on a variety of themes, from the development of a Christian mindset, liturgy, films, to technology and transhumanism. He has a special interest in the relationship between theology and sociology. He also teaches the discipline of Christian Anthropology and the Human Sciences for a postgrad course organized by Christians in the Sciences in Brazil. He supports his much-liked football team Grêmio, loves good coffee, and together with Lili enjoys walking the English footpaths and finding good pubs.

About the Cántaro Institute
Inheriting, Informing, Inspiring

The Cántaro Institute is a confessional evangelical Christian organization established in 2020 that seeks to recover the riches of Spanish Protestantism for the renewal and edification of the contemporary church and to advance the comprehensive Christian philosophy of life for the religious reformation of the Western and Ibero-American world.

We believe that as the Christian church returns to the fount of Scripture as her ultimate authority for all knowing and living, and wisely applies God's truth to every aspect of life, faithful in spirit to the reformers, her missiological activity will result in not only the renewal of the human person but also the reformation of culture, an inevitable result when the true scope and nature of the gospel is made known and applied.

www.ingramcontent.com/pod-product-compliance
Lightning Source LLC
Chambersburg PA
CBHW071419070526
44578CB00003B/610